Quantum Puzzles

Quantum Puzzles

Quirky conundrums to challenge your inner Einstein

Dr Gareth Moore

SIRIUS

SIRIUS

This edition published in 2018 by Sirius Publishing,
a division of Arcturus Publishing Limited,
26/27 Bickels Yard, 151–153 Bermondsey Street,
London SE1 3HA

ISBN: 978-1-78888-411-2
AD006094NT

Printed in China

CONTENTS

Introduction

Pack your lab coat and get ready for a spectacular journey through a cornucopia of science- and technology-based puzzles. With a hugely varied range of challenges, you'll need to stay on your toes if you're going to crack all of the conundrums contained within these pages!

The puzzles are conveniently labelled by scientific discipline as follows:

- **Deductive Logic** – put your brainpower to the test with these deductive reasoning games, making a series of steps on your way to each solution
- **Lateral Hypothesis** – use your creative skills to find an out-of-the-box solution to each of these individual lateral-thinking puzzles
- **Number Crunching** – you'll need your number skills to make sense of these mathematical problems
- **Real Science** – you'll need to use your knowledge of the physical world to solve these fact-based challenges
- **Visual Processing** – these challenges call on your spatial intuition and visual reasoning to help find the unique solution to each logic puzzle

Be sure to check the heading on each page, to see what type of puzzle you are solving. **Deductive Logic** and **Visual Processing** can be solved without any existing skills or experience. **Number Crunching** is similar, but adds in basic maths skills. **Real Science** calls on actual scientific knowledge, although nothing advanced is needed. **Lateral Hypothesis** requires you to come up with a creative solution of your own.
Full solutions are included, although for the **Lateral Hypothesis** puzzles you may come up with good alternatives. The best solution to these is usually the simplest one, however.

Enjoy your adventure!

PUZZLES

LOOP-THE-LAB
VISUAL PROCESSING

The laboratory below consists of a number of tiled floor areas, shown as white squares, and a number of permanent installations, shown as black squares. Can you find a route that visits every white square once and once only, then returns to the starting square? The route can only travel horizontally or vertically between squares.

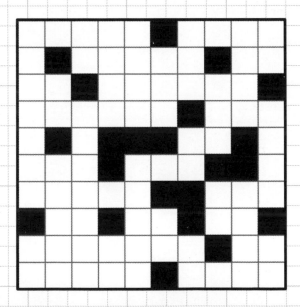

8

ENGINE ROOM
NUMBER CRUNCHING

Two planes are flying across the Atlantic.

The first plane has one engine, and the second plane has two engines. All three engines on the two planes are of the same design, and have a 0.001% chance of failing per flight.

If one of the engines on the two-engine plane fails, the plane will become unbalanced and will be unable to continue flying.

Which plane is safer?

PHIAL FITTING
DEDUCTIVE LOGIC

You have five each of five heights of phial, numbered from 1 (shortest) to 5 (tallest), which must be placed into a 5×5 processing tray in such a way that exactly one of each height of phial appears in every row and column. The phials must be placed according to the numbers outside the tray, each of which indicates the number of phials that can be "seen" from that row/column end. Taller phials obscure shorter ones, so a "3" could clue 13254, with the 1, 3, and 5 phials being visible to give the total of "3."

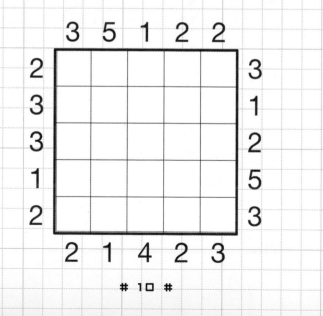

COMPONENT CONNECTION
VISUAL PROCESSING

This electronic breadboard needs to be marked up correctly, ready for the insertion of a series of electronic components. Each component will be placed so that it joins two holes: one white, and one shaded. Can you mark in where all of the components should go? Components can only be placed horizontally or vertically, and cannot cross over one another. All holes are used.

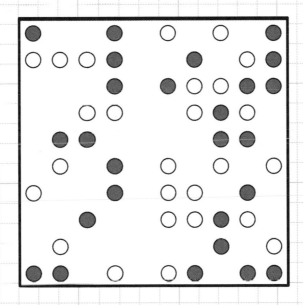

WHEEL PROBLEM
LATERAL HYPOTHESIS

You are in charge of mission control for a Mars mission in which a robot has been flown to Mars in a rocket and is now exploring the planet in a small four-wheeled rover.

The robot needs to get back to the landing site in twenty minutes' time, which is when the rocket has been programmed to fly the robot back to share its findings. On its way back, the robot drives the rover over a sharp piece of rock and punctures a wheel.

You program the robot to remove the four lug nuts attaching the wheel to the car, and then replace it with a new wheel. But a small mistake in your programming causes the robot to knock into the lug nuts so they fly up into the air and float out of the robot's reach.

What's your best chance of getting the robot back to the rocket in time now?

TEST TUBE TEST
DEDUCTIVE LOGIC

A set of test tubes are arranged on a tray as shown. Some of the test tubes need to be filled with wire wool, but not necessarily all the way to the top of the tube. The test tubes are aligned with the grid squares as shown, and must be filled so that any given grid square is either completely filled or completely empty. Numbers outside the tray specify how many grid squares in some rows and columns are to be filled. Test tubes can only be filled from their bottom, marked by the bulb, upward. This means that if any segment other than the bulb is shaded, all the segments from the bulb up to that segment must also be shaded.

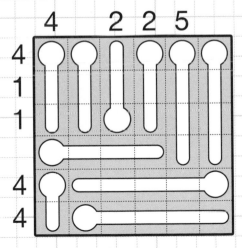

SOCKET PAIRS
VISUAL PROCESSING

The cables are missing between each of these pairs of sockets.
Draw horizontal and vertical lines to indicate the route of each
cable, so that each pair of numbers is linked. For electrical safety
reasons, cables cannot cross either one another or a socket, and
only one cable may enter any square.

	1			2					3
	4		3						
			5				6		
			7	8			8		
	4								5
			9	6			7		
10			2	1					
								9	
					10				

THIN ICE
REAL SCIENCE

Which of the following frozen lake surfaces would it be easier to skate on?

- Ice that is -2°C

- Ice that is -20°C?

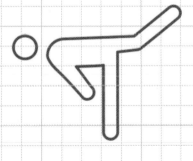

FUEL PODS
VISUAL PROCESSING

The following arrangement of cuboid fuel pods was made by starting from a complete 5×4×4 arrangement of cubes, and then removing some from the top of each stack.

Given that none of the fuel cubes are floating in mid-air, how many fuel cubes are present in the following picture?

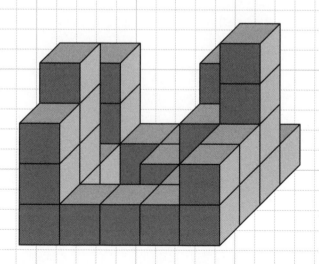

DIFFERENT REACTIONS
DEDUCTIVE LOGIC

You have three solutions:

- One is clear
- One is blue
- One is orange

You test their pH and obtain the following results:

- One is strongly acidic
- One is mildly acidic
- One is mildly alkaline

You then try adding water to them and obtain the following results:

- One has no reaction
- One turns cloudy
- One reacts violently

Given that a) the pH of the blue solution is equivalent to the sum of the pH of the other two solutions, b) the unreactive solution is not clear, and c) the clear solution is less acidic than the one that reacts violently to water, can you deduce which solution has which properties? A pH less than 7 is acidic; a pH greater than 7 is alkaline.

GOOD EGG
REAL SCIENCE

A raw egg in its shell will normally sink in a cup of water.

You, however, wish to make it float. How can you make it do this?

Next, what if you wish it to float halfway between the bottom and the top of the water in the cup?

CELL REJECTION
DEDUCTIVE LOGIC

You need to set up an experiment whereby six different types of cell, A to F, are added to each row and column of a lab tray.

You must ensure that the cells do not interfere with one another. This means that two identical cells cannot be in grid squares that touch, including diagonally.

Can you place a cell into all the empty squares on the tray below?

		E	D		
	B	D	E	C	
A					E

LAB LIGHTS
VISUAL PROCESSING

Can you work out the location of the lights on the lab plan below?
You know that every square of the lab must be illuminated by at
least one light, but also that no light illuminates any other light.
Due to the special lights used, they only light up squares in the
same row or column, and only as far as the first shaded square.
Some shaded squares contain numbers, revealing the number of
lights in the squares immediately to the left, top, right, and bottom.

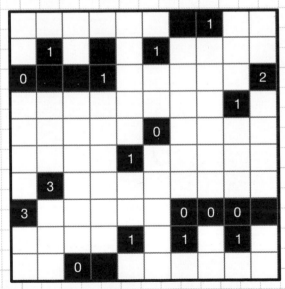

RAISE THE BAR
NUMBER CRUNCHING

You have two solid, cuboid steel bars.

One bar is twice the size of the other in all three dimensions.

How many times heavier is the bigger bar than the smaller bar?

LABORATORY LOGIC
LATERAL HYPOTHESIS

Your lab contains a fume cupboard that is lit by three light bulbs. The control panel for those lights is in the chemical storage room, from which it is not possible to see into the room containing the fume cupboard. All three lights are initially off.

There are three switches, one per light, and you wish to know which switch controls which light. You also want to work this out without visiting the storage room more than once. Given that you do not have anyone else to help you, and you do not have a video monitor or any other device to see the lights from the storage room, how can you do this?

EXPERIMENTAL EXTENSION
NUMBER CRUNCHING

The lead scientist's case load is becoming excessive. Each time he fills a box with case files, he ends up stacking another on top with even more. In fact, each stacked box contains a number of case files equal to the sum of the two boxes immediately below.

Some of the boxes already specify how many case files are contained within that box. Write in the correct number on all of the other boxes too.

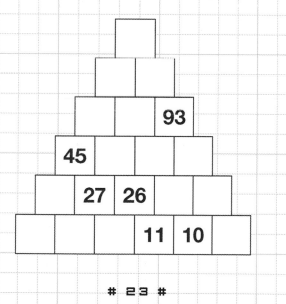

SAMPLE SELECTION
VISUAL PROCESSING

It is your job to fill the specimen tray below so that every square contains one Petri dish. The Petri dishes are of two types, indicated by the white and shaded circles below. All of the Petri dishes of the same type must form a single connected region, so you can travel left/right/up/down from Petri dish to Petri dish. Also, to avoid experimental issues, there can be no 2×2 (or larger) arrangements of Petri dishes of the same type.

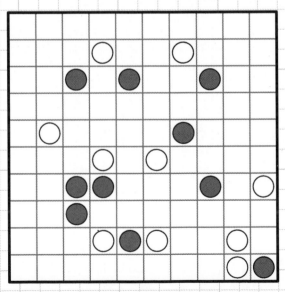

A STRIKING RESULT
LATERAL HYPOTHESIS

You have built a mechanical clock that chimes each hour. At two o'clock, you notice that it takes the clock four seconds to strike the chimes twice, to indicate two. How long do you expect the clock to take to strike the chimes for three? Assume that the duration of each chime is insignficant.

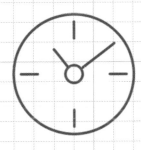

SAILS PITCH
REAL SCIENCE

You are conducting an experiment on the movement of water in the wake of a boat. You have a model boat that is moved by its sails, but inside the lab there is no wind to move the boat along. You do have a small battery-powered fan which could be attached to the back of the boat so that it blows wind into the sails.

Would using this fan help to propel the boat forward?

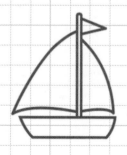

WIRING UP
VISUAL PROCESSING

All of the pins on this board need to be wired up in order to form a continuous loop. The wires should only travel horizontally and vertically between pins, and the wires should not cross at any point. Exactly two wires should connect to each pin. Some pins are already joined with wires.

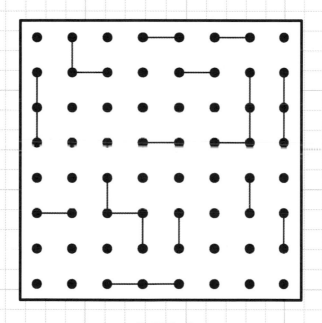

CALCULATOR CONUNDRUM
NUMBER CRUNCHING

You have accidentally spilled glue over your trusty pocket calculator, and now only five keys work: the 9 plus the +, -, ×, and ÷ buttons.

For a very specific experiment, it's essential to display a figure 8 on your calculator display.

What is the simplest way to do this?

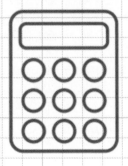

WASTE DISPOSAL
VISUAL PROCESSING

There are two waste disposal chutes in your lab, marked below with black circles. Can you find a route from one to the other? It must travel only horizontally and vertically between squares, and it must never pass within one square of itself, not even diagonally. Numbers outside the grid show how many squares the route visits in a row or column, including the start and end squares.

MIXTURE MIX-UP
NUMBER CRUNCHING

A colleague has set up an experiment using a rack of ten test tubes. Each test tube has a folded piece of card in front of it noting what it contains.

A gust of wind from one of your own experiments knocks all of your colleague's pieces of card onto the floor, so you hastily pick them up and put them back in front of the test tubes before anyone notices. But you have done this randomly, without any actual knowledge of which piece of card belongs where.

What is the probability that **exactly nine** of your pieces of card are in the right place?

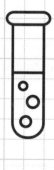

STRANGE ATTRACTORS
VISUAL PROCESSING

Finish routing the particle beam around the lab, forming a loop that passes through the given number of touching and diagonally touching squares next to each numbered attractor. The particles travel only horizontally and vertically, and cannot pass through attractors. The beam cannot re-enter any square.

BINARY CODE
DEDUCTIVE LOGIC

Complete the binary matrix below by writing a "0" or a "1" into each empty square. Each row and column should contain four "0"s and four "1"s, and there should not be more than two "0"s or two "1"s in succession in any row or column.

0				0	0		
		0	1		0		1
	1			1		0	
			0			1	1
1	1			0			
	0		0			1	
1		0		0	1		
		0	0				0

EXPERIMENTAL EXTENSION
NUMBER CRUNCHING

The lead scientist's case load is becoming excessive. Each time he fills a box with case files, he ends up stacking another on top with even more. In fact, each stacked box contains a number of case files equal to the sum of the two boxes immediately below.

Some of the boxes already specify how many case files are contained within that box. Write in the correct number on all of the other boxes too.

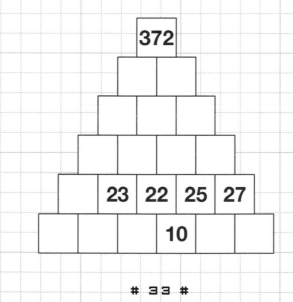

CONNECTED CIRCUIT
DEDUCTIVE LOGIC

Connect all of the circled nodes with horizontal and vertical wires,
so that wires do not cross either each other or another node.
There may be zero, one, or two wires between each pair of nodes.
Each node should have the precise number of wires connected
to it as indicated by its number, and all of the nodes should be
connected so that current can flow from any node to any other
node simply by following one or more wires.

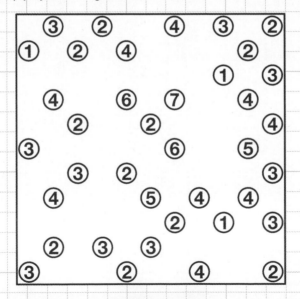

GALACTIC EMPIRE
VISUAL PROCESSING

Each of the planets (indicated by dots) in the grid below controls a region of space that has rotational symmetry around the planet. One is marked as an example. Draw along the dashed grid lines to show the territorial borders of all of the planets. Every square should be in the territory of exactly one planet.

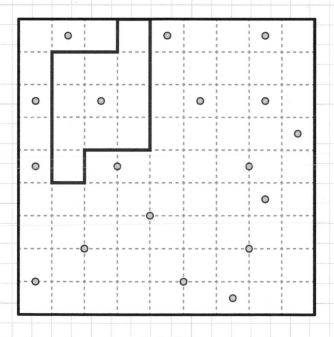

35

LAST MINUTE
LATERAL HYPOTHESIS

You are conducting an experiment that requires you to time a reaction for twelve minutes. Unfortunately, you have only a five-minute hourglass and an eight-minute hourglass to hand.

Is there a way to use these to time twelve minutes, and if so what is it?

PERPLEXING PIPES
VISUAL PROCESSING

The piping system beneath your lab has been only partially constructed. Complete it by drawing in the missing pipes so that every square is connected into the pipe system, and it forms a single loop. Each square contains a corner segment, a straight segment, or a crossing segment. The pipes may only be placed horizontally and vertically, as shown.

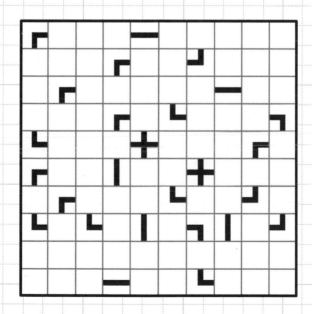

DIFFERENT ATTRACTIONS
DEDUCTIVE LOGIC

You have three magnets of three different strengths. They have three different shapes:

- One is a bar magnet
- One is a horseshoe magnet
- One is a ring magnet

They are made from three different materials:

- One is made from ferrite
- One is made from alnico
- One is made from samarium cobalt

You also know that a) the strongest magnet has a straight edge, b) the horseshoe magnet is weaker than the magnet made from alnico, and c) the material of the medium-strength magnet contains more letters than the material of the horseshoe magnet.

Can you deduce which magnet is made from which material, and how strong they are in comparison to one another?

POWER TRIP
NUMBER CRUNCHING

Your model plane requires four batteries to fly, but the batteries you need come in packs of five. So you decide to get the most out of a pack by rotating which batteries are being used at any one time.

Your batteries finally run out after you've flown your plane for 1,000 minutes.

If all five batteries have been used for the same amount of time, how many minutes long was one battery's life?

PHIAL FITTING
DEDUCTIVE LOGIC

You have five each of five heights of phial, numbered from 1 (shortest) to 5 (tallest), which must be placed into a 5×5 processing tray in such a way that exactly one of each height of phial appears in every row and column. The phials must be placed according to the numbers outside the tray, each of which indicates the number of phials that can be "seen" from that row/column end. Taller phials obscure shorter ones, so a "3" could clue 13254, with the 1, 3, and 5 phials being visible to give the total of "3."

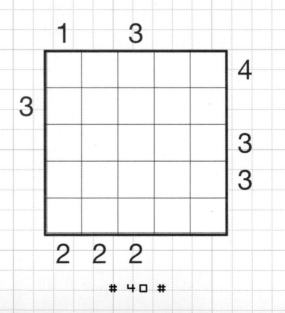

WRAPAROUND WIRING
VISUAL PROCESSING

The cables are missing between each of these pairs of sockets. Draw horizontal and vertical lines to indicate the route of each cable, so that each pair of numbers is linked. For electrical safety reasons, cables cannot cross either one another or a socket, and only one cable may enter any square. Cables may also plug into the edge of the board, in which case they can continue on the opposite end of the same row or column.

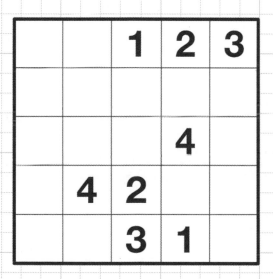

STOP COLD
LATERAL HYPOTHESIS

You are inputting the data from an Arctic expedition into a database and on one particular day of the log you see that the temperature has been recorded as -40 degrees.

However, the explorers recording this data are of various different nationalities, and you don't know whether the person who wrote this intended it to be in degrees Celsius or Fahrenheit.

What do you do?

LAB MICE
VISUAL PROCESSING

You have built a maze to test the very smartest of your tame lab mice. Check that the maze is correctly constructed by finding a route from the entrance at the top to the exit at the bottom.

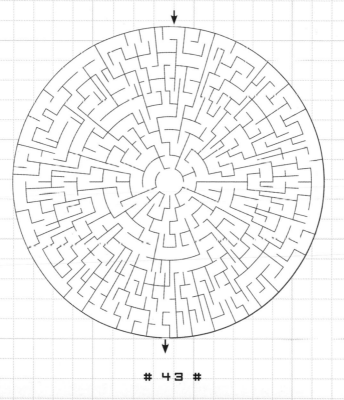

43

SOCKET PAIRS
VISUAL PROCESSING

The cables are missing between each of these pairs of sockets. Draw horizontal and vertical lines to indicate the route of each cable, so that each pair of numbers is linked. For electrical safety reasons, cables cannot cross either one another or a socket, and only one cable may enter any square.

ZERO SUM GAME
NUMBER CRUNCHING

A study reveals that 65% of people cannot do algebra, 70% of people cannot do long division, 75% of people cannot do calculus, and 80% of people cannot calculate percentages.

What is the minimum possible percentage of people that cannot do any of the four?

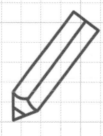

BLACK-OUT EXPERIMENT
DEDUCTIVE LOGIC

A particular experiment requires the careful configuration of six different variables into sets of five items. Add numbers to the diagram below so that each row, column and bold-lined 3×2 box contains five of the numbers in the range 1 to 6, with one per square. Shaded squares are "blacked out" and should not have a number written into them.

COMPONENT CONNECTION
VISUAL PROCESSING

This electronic breadboard needs to be marked up correctly,
ready for the insertion of a series of electronic components. Each
component will be placed so that it joins two holes: one white, and
one shaded. Can you mark in where all of the components should
go? Components can only be placed horizontally or vertically, and
cannot cross over one another. All holes are used.

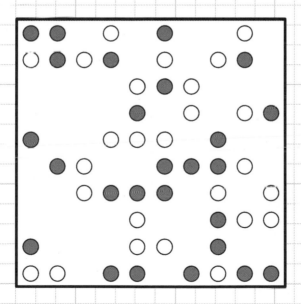

47

UP THE WRONG TREE
LATERAL HYPOTHESIS

You are on an expedition and you discover a circular lake with a radius of 200 meters, which has a small island in the middle. There is a large tree in the island and a large tree on the shore next to the lake. You want to get to the island, but you can't swim. However, you do have a rope which is 205 meters long.

How can you use the rope to get to the middle of the island?

LASER MIRRORS
VISUAL PROCESSING

You have set up a laser experiment, so that a set of lasers are fired through the grid below. Each laser enters and exits at a matching letter, bouncing off the number of mirrors shown. Work out where all of the mirrors should go. There is exactly one per bold-lined region, and it must be at 45 degrees to the horizontal. The bold lines do not affect the path of the lasers.

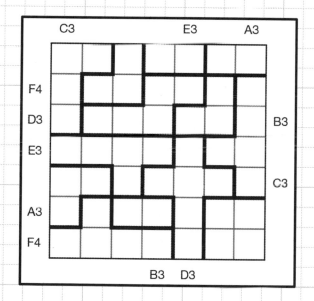

BOTANIC CONFUSION
DEDUCTIVE LOGIC

A number of seeds are located beneath the soil of the plant bed shown below. Can you work out their exact locations? There is no more than one seed per square, and some squares are empty. No seed is in a numbered square. The numbers do, however, indicate the number of squares that contain seeds and which touch, including diagonally.

			1				2
1		2			4	4	
	0		2				1
		1			5		
			2	3			
1		3				2	
	1				0		0
		3					

FREE SPACE
NUMBER CRUNCHING

The current cupboard in the lab doesn't have room for twenty of the lab's beakers. It is replaced with one that is 50% bigger than the original.

Now there is room for twenty more beakers than there are in the lab.

How many beakers are there in the lab?

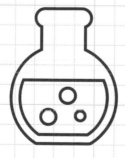

CONNECTED VALUES
NUMBER CRUNCHING

The following experimental grid needs to be completed before
some results can be submitted. Do so by placing a number from
1 to 6 in each square, so each number appears once in every row
and column. Squares with a white dot between them contain two
numbers with a difference of 1. Squares with a black dot between
them contain two numbers where one is twice the value of the
other. All possible dots are shown, except where both are possible
between two squares in which case only one is shown.

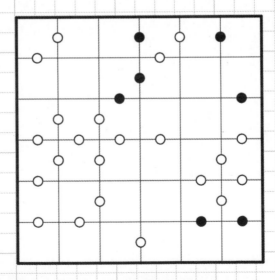

WIRING UP
VISUAL PROCESSING

All of the pins on this board need to be wired up in order to form a continuous loop. The wires should only travel horizontally and vertically between pins, and the wires should not cross at any point. Exactly two wires should connect to each pin. Some pins are already joined with wires.

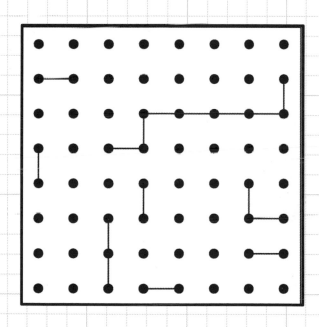

FUEL PODS
VISUAL PROCESSING

The following arrangement of cuboid fuel pods was made by starting from a complete 5×4×4 arrangement of cubes, and then removing some from the top of each stack.

Given that none of the fuel cubes are floating in mid-air, how many fuel cubes are present in the following picture?

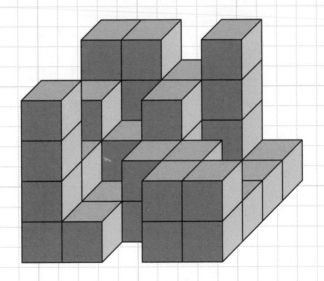

CELL REJECTION
DEDUCTIVE LOGIC

You need to set up an experiment whereby six different types of cell, A to F, are added to each row and column of a lab tray.

You must ensure that the cells do not interfere with one another. This means that two identical cells cannot be in grid squares that touch, including diagonally.

Can you place a cell into all the empty squares on the tray below?

	E			F	
F					D
		F	B		
		E	C		
E					A
	F			E	

LOOP-THE-LAB
VISUAL PROCESSING

The laboratory below consists of a number of tiled floor areas, shown as white squares, and a number of permanent installations, shown as black squares. Can you find a route that visits every white square once and once only, then returns to the starting square? The route can only travel horizontally or vertically between squares.

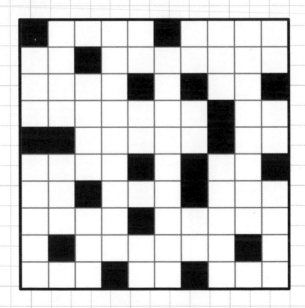

DRIVEN TO DISTRACTION
LATERAL HYPOTHESIS

You and a colleague are driving to a lecture together. You drive for the first twenty kilometers, and then your colleague drives the rest of the way.

On the way back, you take the same route. You drive for the first leg of the return journey, and then your colleague takes over for the last thirty kilometers.

Which of you drives more on this trip, and by how much?

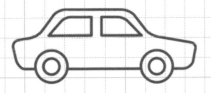

HIDDEN PATH
VISUAL PROCESSING

You have recorded experimental data that reveals the path of
a particular creature as it moves from post to post. It starts at
one of the solid posts, and finishes at the other, moving only
horizontally or vertically between adjoining posts. It does not
cross over any of the shaded squares. Numbers show how many
posts are visited in each row and column. Can you reveal the path?

THE BEETLES
DEDUCTIVE LOGIC

You collect three beetles from your garden. They have three different visual combinations:

- One is red with black spots
- One is yellow with black spots
- One is brown with white spots

They each have a different number of spots:

- One has seven spots
- One has eleven spots
- One has twelve spots

They are each of different lengths:

- One is 6mm long
- One is 8mm long
- One is 9mm long

Given that a) the beetle with eleven spots has an even-numbered length, b) the beetle with twelve spots is smaller than the red beetle, and c) the 6mm beetle has an odd number of black spots, can you deduce which beetle is how long, and how many spots it has?

WEIGHT AND SEE
NUMBER CRUNCHING

You are playing around with a set of weighing scales and you discover that the scale is perfectly balanced when you put three identical bottles of universal indicator on one side and half a pound of iron and a fourth identical bottle of universal indicator on the other side.

How much does a single bottle of universal indicator weigh?

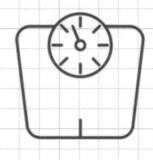

DIAGONAL LINKS
VISUAL PROCESSING

Join each pair of numbers by drawing a set of paths. The paths must be made up of horizontal, vertical, and diagonal segments, and only one path can enter any square. Paths cannot cross, except on the corners between squares where two diagonal paths may cross.

1	2				3
	4	1		2	5
		3		6	
	6				
	7				
4	8		5	7	8

SAMPLE SELECTION
VISUAL PROCESSING

It is your job to fill the specimen tray below so that every square contains one Petri dish. The Petri dishes are of two types, indicated by the white and shaded circles below. All of the Petri dishes of the same type must form a single connected region, so you can travel left/right/up/down from Petri dish to Petri dish. Also, to avoid experimental issues, there can be no 2×2 (or larger) arrangements of Petri dishes of the same type.

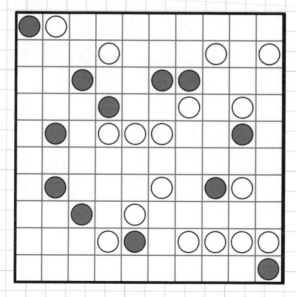

EXPERIMENTAL EXTENSION
NUMBER CRUNCHING

The lead scientist's case load is becoming excessive. Each time he fills a box with case files, he ends up stacking another on top with even more. In fact, each stacked box contains a number of case files equal to the sum of the two boxes immediately below.

Some of the boxes already specify how many case files are contained within that box. Write in the correct number on all of the other boxes too.

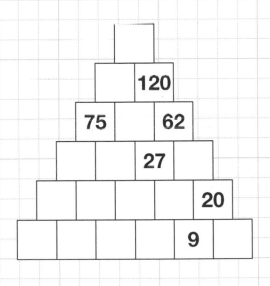

LAB LIGHTS
VISUAL PROCESSING

Can you work out the location of the lights on the lab plan below?
You know that every square of the lab must be illuminated by at
least one light, but also that no light illuminates any other light.
Due to the special lights used, they only light up squares in the
same row or column, and only as far as the first shaded square.
Some shaded squares contain numbers, revealing the number of
lights in the squares immediately to the left, top, right, and bottom.

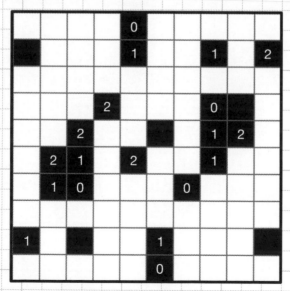

WASTE DISPOSAL
VISUAL PROCESSING

There are two waste disposal chutes in your lab, marked below with black circles. Can you find a route from one to the other? It must travel only horizontally and vertically between squares, and it must never pass within one square of itself, not even diagonally. Numbers outside the grid show how many squares the route visits in a row or column, including the start and end squares.

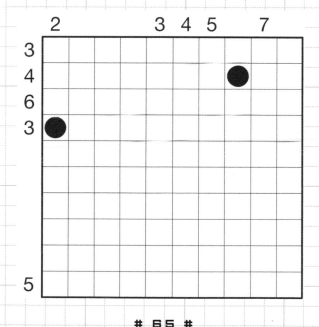

WAXING AND WANING
NUMBER CRUNCHING

You are investigating the chemical properties of wax and you discover that the wax left over from burning four candles can be used to make one more candle. You have a pack of 64 candles.

How many extra candles could you make if you burned all 64 candles?

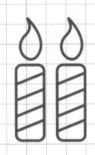

BINARY CODE
DEDUCTIVE LOGIC

Complete the binary matrix below by writing a "0" or a "1" into each empty square. Each row and column should contain four "0"s and four "1"s, and there should not be more than two "0"s or two "1"s in succession in any row or column.

0	0	1	0				
					0	1	
		0		0	1	0	0
0		1		0			
			1		0		1
0	0	1	0		0		
	1	0					
				0	1	0	0

SHAPED CONSTRUCTION
DEDUCTIVE LOGIC

A particular construction requires a very specific arrangement of components, identified by the letters A through G in the diagram below. Write a letter in each of the empty squares so that every row, column, and bold-lined region contains all seven letters exactly once each.

ON ANOTHER PLANET
NUMBER CRUNCHING

Scientists have managed to send a rover to an as yet unexplored planet, and it roves once around the circumference of the planet.

As a result of various obstacles encountered by the rover, they are now planning to send a hovercraft that will hover one meter above the surface of the planet.

If this hovercraft travels once around the circumference of the planet, how much longer (in distance) will its journey around the planet be than the journey of the rover?

CONNECTED CIRCUIT
DEDUCTIVE LOGIC

Connect all of the circled nodes with horizontal and vertical wires,
so that wires do not cross either each other or another node.
There may be zero, one, or two wires between each pair of nodes.
Each node should have the precise number of wires connected
to it as indicated by its number, and all of the nodes should be
connected so that current can flow from any node to any other
node simply by following one or more wires.

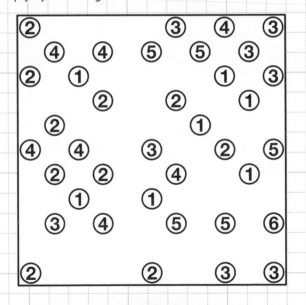

MAGNIFICENT MEASUREMENT
NUMBER CRUNCHING

You are examining some specimens with a magnifying glass that magnifies everything three times.

You have previously measured a 60-degree angle on a piece of paper and you now look at this angle through your magnifying glass.

What size is the magnified angle?

PERPLEXING PIPES
VISUAL PROCESSING

The piping system beneath your lab has been only partially
constructed. Complete it by drawing in the missing pipes so that
every square is connected into the pipe system, and it forms a
single loop. Each square contains a corner segment, a straight
segment, or a crossing segment. The pipes may only be placed
horizontally and vertically, as shown.

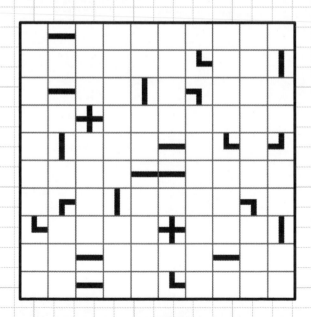

GALACTIC EMPIRE
VISUAL PROCESSING

Each of the planets (indicated by dots) in the grid below controls a region of space that has rotational symmetry around the planet. Draw along the dashed grid lines to show the territorial borders of all of the planets. Every square should be in the territory of exactly one planet. See page 35 for an example region.

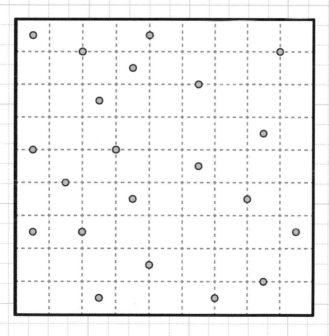

MIX AND MATCH
LATERAL HYPOTHESIS

You have a flask of saline solution and a beaker of distilled water. You pour some of the saline solution into the distilled water, and then some of the resulting mixture back into the flask so that both the flask and the beaker contain the same amount of liquid as they did at the start.

Is there more saline solution in the beaker than distilled water in the flask?

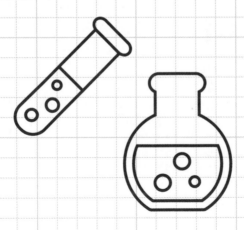

WRAPAROUND WIRING
VISUAL PROCESSING

The cables are missing between each of these pairs of sockets. Draw horizontal and vertical lines to indicate the route of each cable, so that each pair of numbers is linked. For electrical safety reasons, cables cannot cross either one another or a socket, and only one cable may enter any square. Cables may also plug into the edge of the board, in which case they can continue on the opposite end of the same row or column.

	1			
	2	3	2	
3		1		
4				
		4		

BIRD'S-EYE VIEW
REAL SCIENCE

A human being can survive in zero gravity conditions.

However, if you were to send a bird into space to study it under zero gravity conditions, then even if you were to supply it with adequate water for the journey, it would soon die of dehydration.

Why is this?

LASER MIRRORS
VISUAL PROCESSING

You have set up a laser experiment, so that a set of lasers are
fired through the grid below. Each laser enters and exits at a
matching letter, bouncing off the number of mirrors shown. Work
out where all of the mirrors should go. There is exactly one per
bold-lined region, and it must be at 45 degrees to the horizontal.
The bold lines do not affect the path of the lasers.

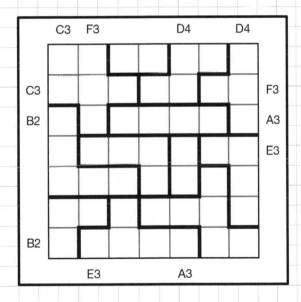

BLACK-OUT EXPERIMENT
DEDUCTIVE LOGIC

A particular experiment requires the careful configuration of six different variables into sets of five items. Add numbers to the diagram below so that each row, column and bold-lined 3×2 box contains five of the numbers in the range 1 to 6, with one per square. Shaded squares are "blacked out" and should not have a number written into them.

AN ALARMING PROBLEM
LATERAL HYPOTHESIS

You have built yourself a wind-up alarm clock. At nine p.m., you go to bed, and you wind your alarm clock and set it for noon. You then fall asleep almost immediately.

How much sleep have you had when the alarm wakes you up?

STRANGE ATTRACTORS
VISUAL PROCESSING

Draw the route of a particle beam around the lab below, forming a loop that passes through the given number of touching and diagonally touching squares next to each numbered attractor. The particles travel only horizontally and vertically, and cannot pass through attractors. The beam cannot re-enter any square.

	3		4				
						8	
5				7			5
				7			
		6					
		6				8	

PERFECT MATCH
LATERAL HYPOTHESIS

You have a book of paper matches. You take one out, throw it into the air, and, unsurprisingly, it lands on its flat side. Then you do something to the match so that the next time you throw it into the air it lands on its edge.

How is this possible?

CONNECTED VALUES
NUMBER CRUNCHING

The following experimental grid needs to be completed before some results can be submitted. Do so by placing a number from 1 to 6 in each square, so each number appears once in every row and column. Squares with a white dot between them contain two numbers with a difference of 1. Squares with a black dot between them contain two numbers where one is twice the value of the other. All possible dots are shown, except where both are possible between two squares in which case only one is shown.

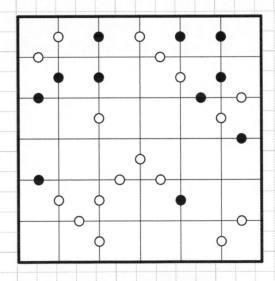

82

THEIR LAST LEGS
NUMBER CRUNCHING

A tripod has three legs and a clamp stand has one leg.

If your tripod and clamp stand cupboard contains 13 pieces of equipment and 33 legs, how many tripods and clamp stands do you have?

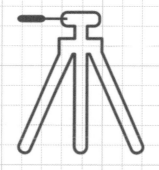

SQUARE ROOMS
VISUAL PROCESSING

Divide the lab floor up into a series of square rooms, so that each room contains a single circular console. All squares should form part of exactly one room.

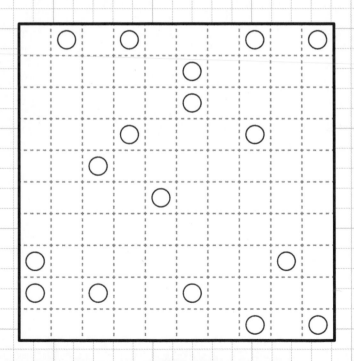

STONE COLD
REAL SCIENCE

The central heating in your house ensures that it is the same temperature in every room.

However, whenever you use the bathroom at night, you notice that the tiled floor of the bathroom is much colder on your bare feet than the carpeted floor of your bedroom and hallway.

Why is this so?

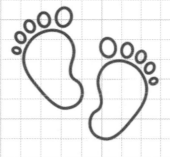

PHIAL FITTING
DEDUCTIVE LOGIC

You have five each of five heights of phial, numbered from
1 (shortest) to 5 (tallest), which must be placed into a 5×5
processing tray in such a way that exactly one of each height of
phial appears in every row and column. The phials must be placed
according to the numbers outside the tray, each of which indicates
the number of phials that can be "seen" from that row/column
end. Taller phials obscure shorter ones, so a "3" could clue 13254,
with the 1, 3, and 5 phials being visible to give the total of "3."

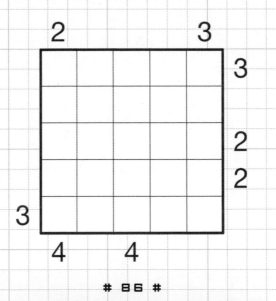

DROPPING OFF
NUMBER CRUNCHING

You are dropping hydrochloric acid into a row of test tubes.

You drop one drop in the first test tube, and in every subsequent test tube you drop more drops than the previous one.

Once you've reached the end of the row, you have dropped 100 drops of hydrochloric acid.

What is the largest number of test tubes that could have been filled in the row?

HIDDEN PATH
VISUAL PROCESSING

You have experimental recordings that reveal the path of a certain creature as it moves from post to post. It starts at one of the solid posts, and finishes at the other, moving only horizontally or vertically between adjoining posts. It does not cross over any of the shaded squares. Numbers show how many posts are visited in some rows and columns. Can you reveal the path?

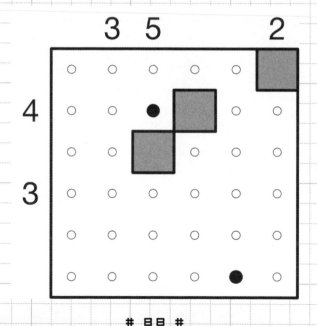

PLANE SAILING
REAL SCIENCE

A plane stalls, and begins to plummet into a nosedive. The pilot tries to pull out of the dive immediately, but is unsuccessful.

After the plane has been nosediving for some time, the pilot tries again, and this time he is able to pull out of the dive.

Why is it easier for him to pull out of a nosedive after the plane has been diving for some time?

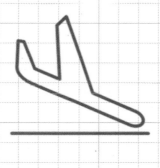

SHAPED CONSTRUCTION
DEDUCTIVE LOGIC

A particular construction requires a very specific arrangement of components, identified by the letters A through G in the diagram below. Write a letter in each of the empty squares so that every row, column, and bold-lined region contains all seven letters exactly once each.

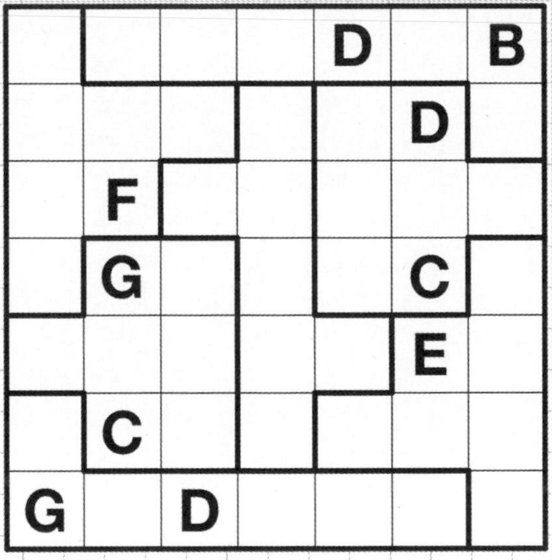

TALKING SENSE
REAL SCIENCE

It sometimes said that you have two eyes and two ears but only one mouth because you ought to look and listen more than you speak.

But what is the biological explanation for this phenomenon?

SOCKET PAIRS
VISUAL PROCESSING

The cables are missing between each of these pairs of sockets. Draw horizontal and vertical lines to indicate the route of each cable, so that each pair of numbers is linked. For electrical safety reasons, cables cannot cross either one another or a socket, and only one cable may enter any square.

					1			
2	3				4		5	
	6			3				7
					4			
	8							
9		10			2			
						5		
	6		10		7	9	1	
8								

CATCH YOUR BREATH
REAL SCIENCE

You are on a scuba diving expedition. You have swum down to the bottom of the ocean and are examining some coral when you realize that your tank has stopped working.

In order to make it back to the surface, you will have to swim upward rapidly, and hope that the air in your lungs is enough to get you all the way there.

Should you hold your breath as you swim upward, or should you gradually let the air escape your mouth?

LAB MICE
VISUAL PROCESSING

You have built a maze to test the very smartest of your tame lab mice. Check that the maze is correctly constructed by finding a route from the entrance at the top to the exit at the bottom.

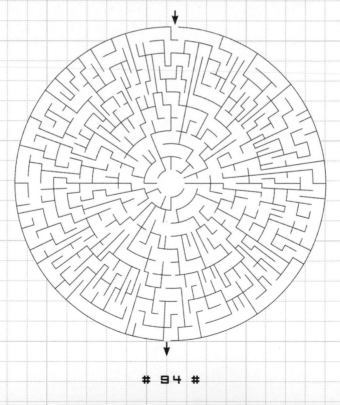

94

ROUND TRIP
REAL SCIENCE

Imagine that you have a free-standing rotating mirror.

A fly starts flying around the mirror and it flies at a speed that makes its image in the mirror appear to be stationary.

What must the relationship between the speed of the fly and the speed of the mirror be to achieve this effect?

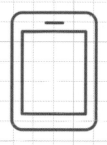

FUEL PODS
VISUAL PROCESSING

The following arrangement of cuboid fuel pods was made by starting from a complete 5×4×4 arrangement of cubes, and then removing some from the top of each stack.

Given that none of the fuel cubes are floating in mid-air, how many fuel cubes are present in the following picture?

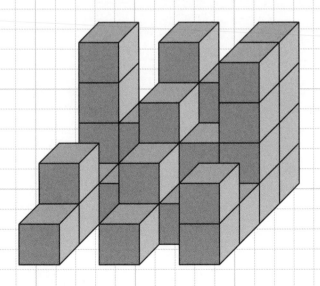

JUST GRADUATED
NUMBER CRUNCHING

You accidentally drop a graduated cylinder into a tub containing three liters of distilled water, so that the fifteen milliliter mark on the cylinder is at water level.

You then add another half a liter of water to the tub, ensuring that none goes into the cylinder.

Which part of the cylinder is at water level now?

LOOP-THE-LAB
VISUAL PROCESSING

The laboratory below consists of a number of tiled floor areas, shown as white squares, and a number of permanent installations, shown as black squares. Can you find a route that visits every white square once and once only, then returns to the starting square? The route can only travel horizontally or vertically between squares.

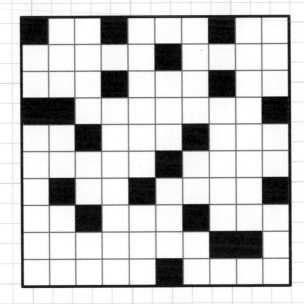

98

BURST YOUR BUBBLES
REAL SCIENCE

You are on a caving expedition, and you and your fellow cavers have succeeded in your aim to reach a very deep cave that has never been reached by anyone before.

You have brought a bottle of cava with you to celebrate this achievement and you open it, but to your disappointment the bottle hardly pops, and the cava is flat.

However, when you return above ground, you all feel nauseous.

What has caused this to happen?

SQUARE ROOMS
VISUAL PROCESSING

Divide the lab floor up into a series of square rooms, so that each room contains a single circular console. All squares should form part of exactly one room.

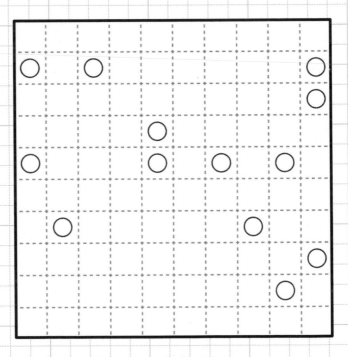

100

DIAGONAL LINKS
VISUAL PROCESSING

Join each pair of numbers by drawing a set of paths. The paths must be made up of horizontal, vertical, and diagonal segments, and only one path can enter any square. Paths cannot cross, except on the corners between squares where two diagonal paths may cross.

1	2		1		3
					4
					5
3				6	
6	4			5	2

FACE THE MUSIC
REAL SCIENCE

If you wet your finger and slide it round the rim of a wine glass at just the right speed, a singing noise will start to emanate from the glass.

What makes this happen? And why does your finger need to be wet for it to work?

WASTE DISPOSAL
VISUAL PROCESSING

There are two waste disposal chutes in your lab, marked below with black circles. Can you find a route from one to the other? It must travel only horizontally and vertically between squares, and it must never pass within one square of itself, not even diagonally. Numbers outside the grid show how many squares the route visits in a row or column, including the start and end squares.

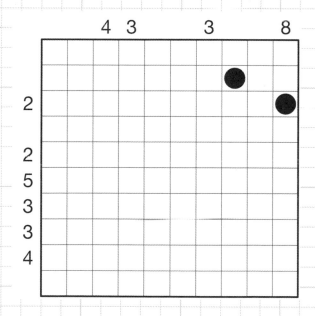

CONNECTED CIRCUIT
DEDUCTIVE LOGIC

Connect all of the circled nodes with horizontal and vertical wires,
so that wires do not cross either each other or another node.
There may be zero, one, or two wires between each pair of nodes.
Each node should have the precise number of wires connected
to it as indicated by its number, and all of the nodes should be
connected so that current can flow from any node to any other
node simply by following one or more wires.

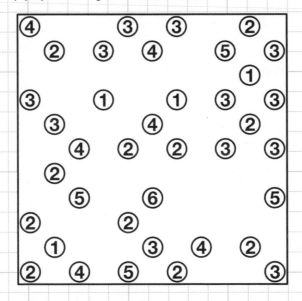

104

HOUSE-WARMING PARTY
LATERAL HYPOTHESIS

Your colleague is showing you some work he has been doing to develop more efficient methods of home insulation.

"There's still work to do," he says, "but ultimately I intend to halve the percentage heat loss of your average house."

"That's impossible!" you reply.

Why?

STRANGE ATTRACTORS
VISUAL PROCESSING

Draw the route of a particle beam around the lab below, forming a loop that passes through the given number of touching and diagonally touching squares next to each numbered attractor. The particles travel only horizontally and vertically, and cannot pass through attractors. The beam cannot re-enter any square.

				5		
		6				
4						
	7					5
3				7		
4		8				
				8		
		5				

SNOW BUSINESS
REAL SCIENCE

When it snows, the world gets quieter.

People stay indoors, and there is less traffic on the roads.

But there's also a scientific reason why snowfall makes things quieter.

What is it?

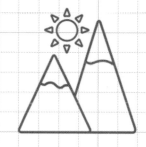

SHAPED CONSTRUCTION
DEDUCTIVE LOGIC

A particular construction requires a very specific arrangement of components, identified by the letters A through G in the diagram below. Write a letter in each of the empty squares so that every row, column, and bold-lined region contains all seven letters exactly once each.

BUNSEN SQUARES
VISUAL PROCESSING

Nine Bunsen burners are laid out in three rows of three as shown below. A large square of tape has been placed around them. Now can you add two more squares of tape so that each Bunsen burner ends up in a separate area of its own, surrounded entirely by tape on all sides?

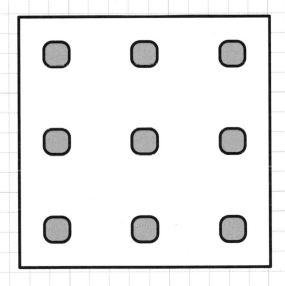

LAB LIGHTS
VISUAL PROCESSING

Can you work out the location of the lights on the lab plan below? You know that every square of the lab must be illuminated by at least one light, but also that no light illuminates any other light. Due to the special lights used, they only light up squares in the same row or column, and only as far as the first shaded square. Some shaded squares contain numbers, revealing the number of lights in the squares immediately to the left, top, right, and bottom.

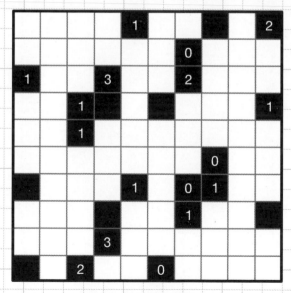

IN HOT WATER
REAL SCIENCE

A boiling kettle can be quite noisy, and some kettles will even whistle or sing as they approach the boil.

What causes this noise?

And why does the noise stop just before the kettle reaches the boil?

LOOP-THE-LAB
VISUAL PROCESSING

The laboratory below consists of a number of tiled floor areas, shown as white squares, and a number of permanent installations, shown as black squares. Can you find a route that visits every white square once and once only, then returns to the starting square? The route can only travel horizontally or vertically between squares.

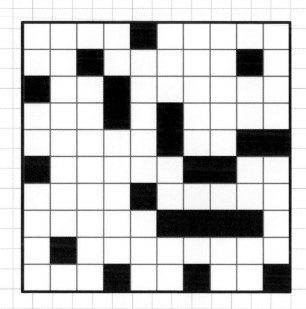

FIND YOUR VOICE
REAL SCIENCE

Almost everyone hates the sound of their own voice when they hear it played back to them on a recording.

But when other people hear your voice on a recording they say it sounds normal.

Why might this be?

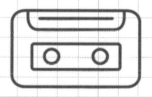

SAMPLE SELECTION
VISUAL PROCESSING

It is your job to fill the specimen tray below so that every square contains one Petri dish. The Petri dishes are of two types, indicated by the white and shaded circles below. All of the Petri dishes of the same type must form a single connected region, so you can travel left/right/up/down from Petri dish to Petri dish. Also, to avoid experimental issues, there can be no 2×2 (or larger) arrangements of Petri dishes of the same type.

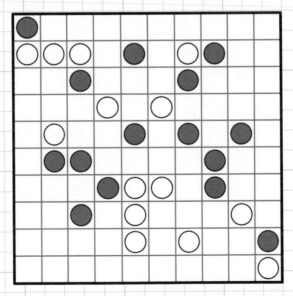

ROCK FAN

DEDUCTIVE LOGIC

You are a geologist and you have been studying three rocks of different weights. The rocks are of different types:

- One is igneous

- One is metamorphic

- One is sedimentary

You have studied one rock per day:

- One on Monday

- One on Tuesday

- One on Wednesday

Given that a) you studied the metamorphic rock the day before you studied the lightest rock, and b) the igneous rock is heavier than the rock you studied on Monday, can you deduce which type of rock you studied on which day, and their comparative weights?

ON THE MAP
LATERAL HYPOTHESIS

You are planning a hiking trip with your friend.

You buy a map of the region, but when you meet up with your friend you discover he has also bought a map, only it is a much bigger version of yours.

He puts his map down on the table and you put yours so its entirety is on top of his.

Is there any guarantee that there is a point on your smaller map which is on top of exactly the same point on the bigger map?

CELL REJECTION
DEDUCTIVE LOGIC

You need to set up an experiment whereby six different types of cell, A to F, are added to each row and column of a lab tray.

You must ensure that the cells do not interfere with one another. This means that two identical cells cannot be in grid squares that touch, including diagonally.

Can you place a cell into all the empty squares on the tray below?

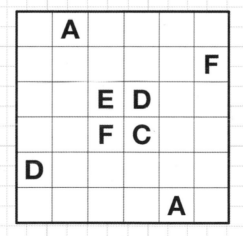

WIRING UP
VISUAL PROCESSING

All of the pins on this board need to be wired up in order to form a continuous loop. The wires should only travel horizontally and vertically between pins, and the wires should not cross at any point. Exactly two wires should connect to each pin. Some pins are already joined with wires.

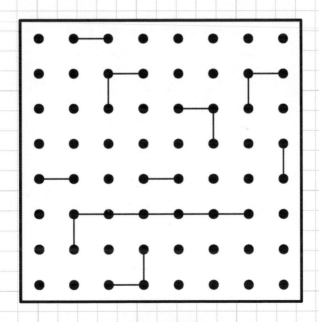

BREAK THE ICE
REAL SCIENCE

You have been pouring drinks for a party and, as it's a hot day, you decide to pop some ice cubes in them.

As the ice cubes enter the drinks they make a cracking sound.

Why does this happen, rather than the cubes just melting?

BINARY CODE
DEDUCTIVE LOGIC

Complete the binary matrix below by writing a "0" or a "1" into
each empty square. Each row and column should contain four
"0"s and four "1"s, and there should not be more than two "0"s or
two "1"s in succession in any row or column.

	0	1			0	1	1
1	1			1			
0			1		1	1	
	1		1		1	0	
	0	1		1		1	
	0	1		0			0
			1			0	0
0	1	0			0	1	

COMPONENT CONNECTION
VISUAL PROCESSING

This electronic breadboard needs to be marked up correctly, ready for the insertion of a series of electronic components. Each component will be placed so that it joins two holes: one white, and one shaded. Can you mark in where all of the components should go? Components can only be placed horizontally or vertically, and cannot cross over one another. All holes are used.

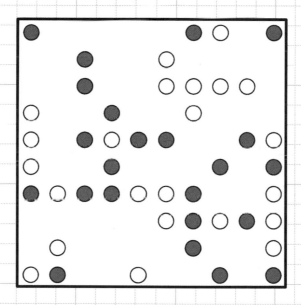

KIDDING AROUND
NUMBER CRUNCHING

You are talking to two of your colleagues about their children.
First, you talk to Alice:

- She has two children

- They are not both girls

What is the probability that they are both boys?

Second, you talk to Ben:

- Ben has two children

- The youngest is a boy

What is the probability that they are both boys?

EXPERIMENTAL EXTENSION
NUMBER CRUNCHING

The lead scientist's case load is becoming excessive. Each time he fills a box with case files, he ends up stacking another on top with even more. In fact, each stacked box contains a number of case files equal to the sum of the two boxes immediately below.

Some of the boxes already specify how many case files are contained within that box. Write in the correct number on all of the other boxes too.

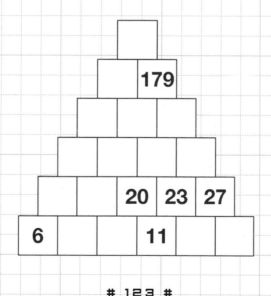

DIAGONAL LINKS
VISUAL PROCESSING

Join each pair of numbers by drawing a set of paths. The paths must be made up of horizontal, vertical, and diagonal segments, and only one path can enter any square. Paths cannot cross, except on the corners between squares where two diagonal paths may cross.

1	2			3	4
	4				
5					
1	2		3		
6		5			6

DROP BY DROP
NUMBER CRUNCHING

You are running an experiment in June.

On the first of June, you drop one drop of acid into a solution.

On the second, you drop two, on the third three, and so on until the 30th, on which you drop 30 drops.

On which day do you drop the 200th drop?

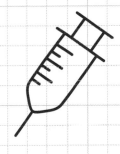

GALACTIC EMPIRE
VISUAL PROCESSING

Each of the planets (indicated by dots) in the grid below controls a region of space that has rotational symmetry around the planet. Draw along the dashed grid lines to show the territorial borders of all of the planets. Every square should be in the territory of exactly one planet. See page 35 for an example region.

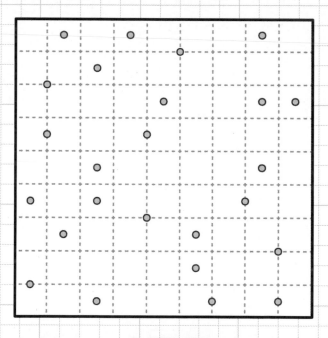

EARWIGGING

LATERAL HYPOTHESIS

You are running an experiment on earwigs, so you have collected a large number of them in a big crate.

You think you have a few hundred and you want to verify that, but it's impossible to count them as they keep moving around.

How might you get a reasonably accurate estimate?

PERPLEXING PIPES
VISUAL PROCESSING

The piping system beneath your lab has been only partially constructed. Complete it by drawing in the missing pipes so that every square is connected into the pipe system, and it forms a single loop. Each square contains a corner segment, a straight segment, or a crossing segment. The pipes may only be placed horizontally and vertically, as shown.

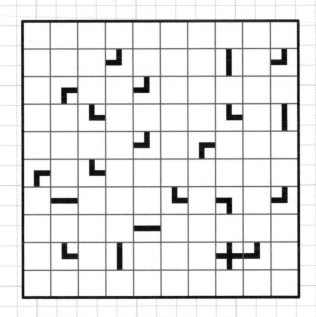

THE LATE REPORT
NUMBER CRUNCHING

You need to write up a 4,000 word report for a deadline, and you calculate that if you write 200 words a day you'll finish it just in time.

However, you have a number of exciting experiments on the go, and you discover that you are only able to write the first half of the report at a rate of 100 words a day.

Will upping your output to 300 words a day for the second half of the report allow you to finish it in time?

WRAPAROUND WIRING
VISUAL PROCESSING

The cables are missing between each of these pairs of sockets. Draw horizontal and vertical lines to indicate the route of each cable, so that each pair of numbers is linked. For electrical safety reasons, cables cannot cross either one another or a socket, and only one cable may enter any square. Cables may also plug into the edge of the board, in which case they can continue on the opposite end of the same row or column.

1	2	3		2
				4
	3			
			1	4

THE BREAKDOWN
NUMBER CRUNCHING

Decomposer A and decomposer B together break down a substance in ten minutes.

But the two decomposers work at different speeds.

Decomposer A could have broken down that same substance by itself in fifteen minutes.

How long would it have taken for decomposer B to break down the substance on its own?

LASER MIRRORS
VISUAL PROCESSING

You have set up a laser experiment, so that a set of lasers are fired through the grid below. Each laser enters and exits at a matching letter, bouncing off the number of mirrors shown. Work out where all of the mirrors should go. There is exactly one per bold-lined region, and it must be at 45 degrees to the horizontal. The bold lines do not affect the path of the lasers.

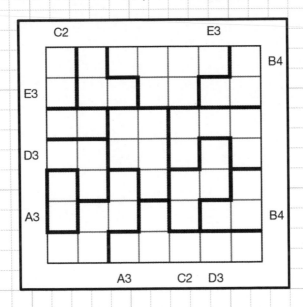

TIME AFTER TIME
NUMBER CRUNCHING

The hour hand of a clock is six centimeters long, and the minute hand is nine centimeters long.

How much faster does the tip of the minute hand move than the tip of the hour hand?

BLACK-OUT EXPERIMENT
DEDUCTIVE LOGIC

A particular experiment requires the careful configuration of six different variables into sets of five items. Add numbers to the diagram below so that each row, column and bold-lined 3×2 box contains five of the numbers in the range 1 to 6, with one per square. Shaded squares are "blacked out" and should not have a number written into them.

				5	6
	3	1		4	
			3	1	
	5	6			1
3				2	

134

LAB MICE
VISUAL PROCESSING

You have built a maze to test the very smartest of your tame lab mice. Check that the maze is correctly constructed by finding a route from the entrance at the top to the exit at the bottom.

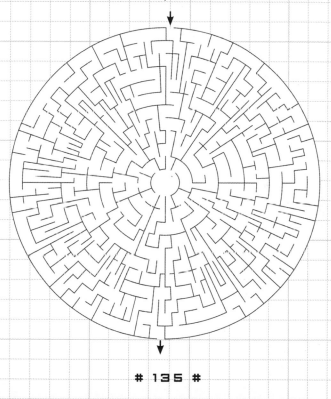

SQUARE ROOMS
VISUAL PROCESSING

Divide the lab floor up into a series of square rooms, so that each room contains a single circular console. All squares should form part of exactly one room.

HIDDEN PATH
VISUAL PROCESSING

You have experimental recordings that reveal the path of a certain creature as it moves from post to post. It starts at one of the solid posts, and finishes at the other, moving only horizontally or vertically between adjoining posts. It does not cross over any of the shaded squares. Numbers show how many posts are visited in some rows and columns. Can you reveal the path?

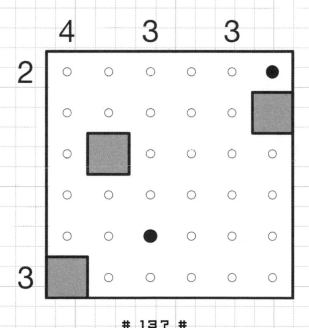

FULL CIRCLE
LATERAL HYPOTHESIS

Take a regular, two-dimensional circle. With three cuts, and no
rearrangement of the pieces after they have been cut, what is the
largest number of pieces you can make?

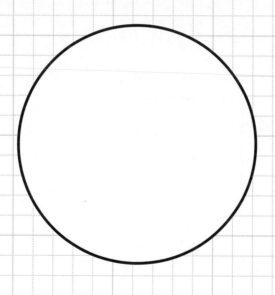

SPONGE AWAY
NUMBER CRUNCHING

You buy a sponge.

The packet says that when the sponge has absorbed the maximum amount of liquid it can hold, it is 99% liquid.

After a spillage in the lab, you use the sponge to mop up a solution until the sponge is incapable of absorbing any more liquid.

You weigh the wet sponge and then wring it out until it only weighs half as much.

What percentage of the sponge's weight is liquid now?

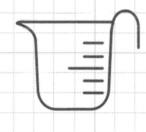

DOUBLE TIME
NUMBER CRUNCHING

On New Year's Day you purchase an ant farm whose population doubles every month.

By the first of July the farm is half full.

When will the farm be completely full?

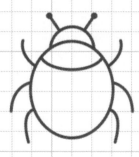

CONNECTED VALUES
NUMBER CRUNCHING

The following experimental grid needs to be completed before some results can be submitted. Do so by placing a number from 1 to 6 in each square, so each number appears once in every row and column. Squares with a white dot between them contain two numbers with a difference of 1. Squares with a black dot between them contain two numbers where one is twice the value of the other. All possible dots are shown, except where both are possible between two squares in which case only one is shown.

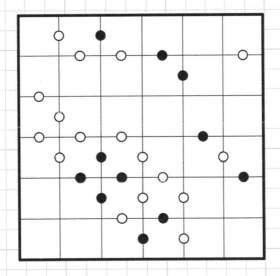

SHAPED CONSTRUCTION
DEDUCTIVE LOGIC

A particular construction requires a very specific arrangement of components, identified by the letters A through G in the diagram below. Write a letter in each of the empty squares so that every row, column, and bold-lined region contains all seven letters exactly once each.

G						
A				G	E	
		F			B	
	B			A		
	G	C				A
						F

ADVANCED ROBOTICS
DEDUCTIVE LOGIC

You are repairing three robots. Their names are:

- Cog
- Circuit
- Bolt

The robots have three different liveries:

- One is red
- One is gold
- One is silver

They each need a different number of parts:

- One needs two parts
- One needs three parts
- One needs four parts

Given that a) no robot needs the same number of parts as letters in its name, b) the gold robot needs more parts than Cog, and c) Circuit needs as many parts as letters in the red robot's name, can you deduce which robot has which livery, and how many parts they each need?

THE WEIGHT IS OVER
NUMBER CRUNCHING

A piece of iron weighs 72 grams plus one fifth of its weight.

How much does it weigh in total?

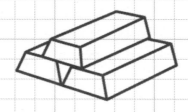

WIRING UP
VISUAL PROCESSING

All of the pins on this board need to be wired up in order to form a continuous loop. The wires should only travel horizontally and vertically between pins, and the wires should not cross at any point. Exactly two wires should connect to each pin. Some pins are already joined with wires.

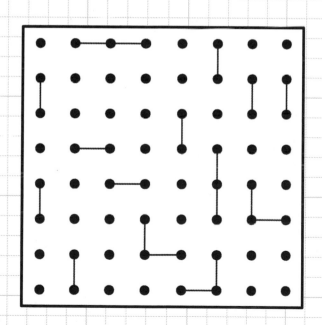

PHIAL FITTING
DEDUCTIVE LOGIC

You have five each of five heights of phial, numbered from
1 (shortest) to 5 (tallest), which must be placed into a 5×5
processing tray in such a way that exactly one of each height of
phial appears in every row and column. The phials must be placed
according to the numbers outside the tray, each of which indicates
the number of phials that can be "seen" from that row/column
end. Taller phials obscure shorter ones, so a "3" could clue 13254,
with the 1, 3, and 5 phials being visible to give the total of "3."

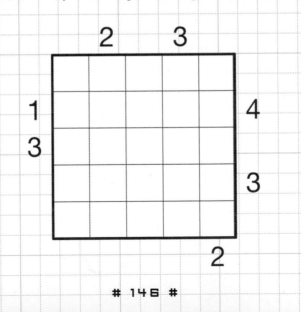

MEASURE FOR MEASURE
LATERAL HYPOTHESIS

You get through a bottle of universal indicator once every fortnight.

The lab shops for supplies every Saturday, so if you'll need a new bottle before next Saturday, you'll have to put your order in.

However, you don't have any measuring equipment to hand.

How can you work out whether your bottle is at least half full without any measuring equipment?

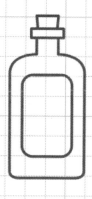

SQUARE ROOMS
VISUAL PROCESSING

Divide the lab floor up into a series of square rooms, so that each room contains a single circular console. All squares should form part of exactly one room.

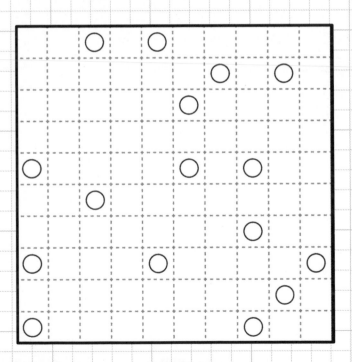

THE NEXT GENERATION
NUMBER CRUNCHING

You have three generators that together generate three kilojoules of energy in three seconds.

You want to generate ten kilojoules in ten seconds. How many more generators do you need?

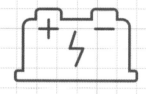

DIAGONAL LINKS
VISUAL PROCESSING

Join each pair of numbers by drawing a set of paths. The paths must be made up of horizontal, vertical, and diagonal segments, and only one path can enter any square. Paths cannot cross, except on the corners between squares where two diagonal paths may cross.

1	2			3	4
			5		
4					2
	1				5
6	3				6

RED LIGHT
REAL SCIENCE

Often when photographs are taken with flash, people's eyes come out red.

What causes this? And how might it be avoided?

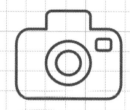

SAMPLE SELECTION
VISUAL PROCESSING

It is your job to fill the specimen tray below so that every square contains one Petri dish. The Petri dishes are of two types, indicated by the white and shaded circles below. All of the Petri dishes of the same type must form a single connected region, so you can travel left/right/up/down from Petri dish to Petri dish. Also, to avoid experimental issues, there can be no 2×2 (or larger) arrangements of Petri dishes of the same type.

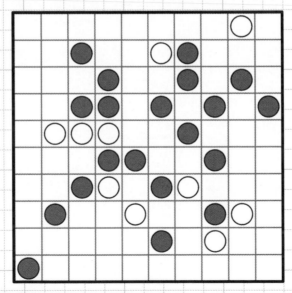

HIDDEN PATH
VISUAL PROCESSING

You have experimental recordings that reveal the path of a certain creature as it moves from post to post. It starts at one of the solid posts, and finishes at the other, moving only horizontally or vertically between adjoining posts. It does not cross over any of the shaded squares. Numbers show how many posts are visited in some rows and columns. Can you reveal the path?

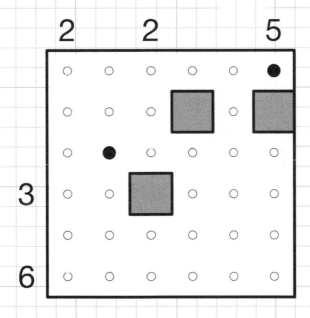

153

CHEMICAL SEPARATION
LATERAL HYPOTHESIS

You have a rack of ten test tubes.

The first five are filled with solution and the second five are empty.

By touching only two test tubes, can you make it so that the tubes alternate between full and empty?

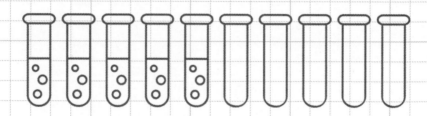

CONNECTED VALUES
NUMBER CRUNCHING

The following experimental grid needs to be completed before some results can be submitted. Do so by placing a number from 1 to 6 in each square, so each number appears once in every row and column. Squares with a white dot between them contain two numbers with a difference of 1. Squares with a black dot between them contain two numbers where one is twice the value of the other. All possible dots are shown, except where both are possible between two squares in which case only one is shown.

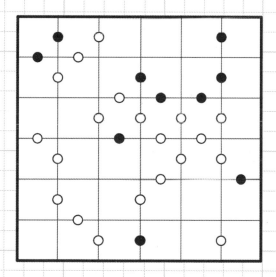

SOCKET PAIRS
VISUAL PROCESSING

The cables are missing between each of these pairs of sockets.
Draw horizontal and vertical lines to indicate the route of each
cable, so that each pair of numbers is linked. For electrical safety
reasons, cables cannot cross either one another or a socket, and
only one cable may enter any square.

			1					
	2			3				
		4		5				1
				6		7		8
5							3	
2	9						10	
				6				
	9						10	
			4	8	7			

LIGHT FLASK

LATERAL HYPOTHESIS

What can you put in an empty flask to make it weigh less?

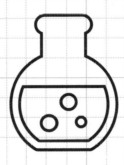

LASER MIRRORS
VISUAL PROCESSING

You have set up a laser experiment, so that a set of lasers are fired through the grid below. Each laser enters and exits at a matching letter, bouncing off the number of mirrors shown. Work out where all of the mirrors should go. There is exactly one per bold-lined region, and it must be at 45 degrees to the horizontal. The bold lines do not affect the path of the lasers.

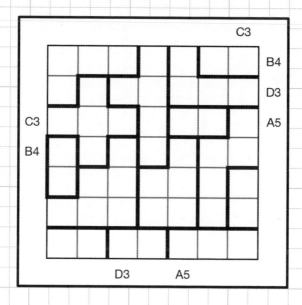

ALIEN NATIONS
DEDUCTIVE LOGIC

You are organizing an interplanetary space summit. Three non-human races will be attending:

- The Sarpons
- The Melluans
- The Arrati

These three races all have a different number of eyes:

- One has no eyes
- One has two eyes
- One has three eyes

They also all have a different number of arms:

- One has one arm
- One has two arms
- One has three arms

Given that a) no race has the same number of arms as eyes, b) the Arrati have more eyes than the one-armed race, and c) the eyeless race have more arms than the Sarpons, can you deduce how many eyes and arms each race has?

TOP SCIENTISTS
NUMBER CRUNCHING

A survey of all the scientists in your lab reveals that 80% of them believe they have carried out more experiments than average for the lab this year.

Is it possible that they're all right?

COMPONENT CONNECTION
VISUAL PROCESSING

This electronic breadboard needs to be marked up correctly, ready for the insertion of a series of electronic components. Each component will be placed so that it joins two holes: one white, and one shaded. Can you mark in where all of the components should go? Components can only be placed horizontally or vertically, and cannot cross over one another. All holes are used.

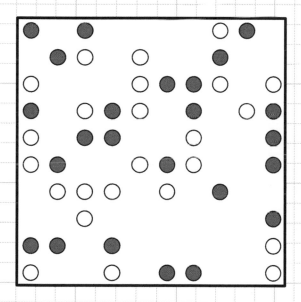

THE LONG WORM
NUMBER CRUNCHING

You are working on a growth hormone and accidentally spill some of it on the floor. A five centimeter-long worm wriggles over it. Initially it appears to be unaffected, but you eventually realize that it is growing, and its rate of growth is increasing. In fact, the worm is doubling in length every day.

After ten days, is the worm closest in length to:

- Two tennis rackets, or

- Two tennis players, or

- Two tennis nets, or

- Two tennis courts?

WASTE DISPOSAL
VISUAL PROCESSING

There are two waste disposal chutes in your lab, marked below with black circles. Can you find a route from one to the other? It must travel only horizontally and vertically between squares, and it must never pass within one square of itself, not even diagonally. Numbers outside the grid show how many squares the route visits in a row or column, including the start and end squares.

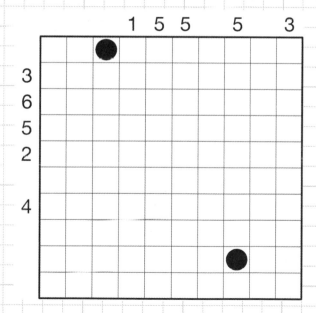

FUEL PODS
VISUAL PROCESSING

The following arrangement of cuboid fuel pods was made by starting from a complete 5×4×4 arrangement of cubes, and then removing some from the top of each stack.

Given that none of the fuel cubes are floating in mid-air, how many fuel cubes are present in the following picture?

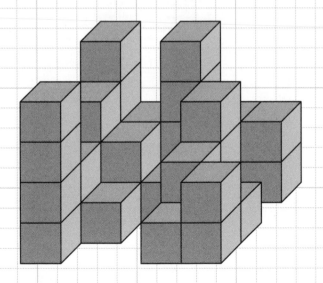

THE STRONGEST ACID
LATERAL HYPOTHESIS

One of your colleagues shows you a flask of a strange liquid.

He claims it is an acid so strong it can eat through anything.

Is this possible?

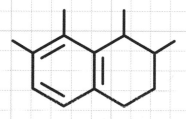

STRANGE ATTRACTORS
VISUAL PROCESSING

Draw the route of a particle beam around the lab below, forming a loop that passes through the given number of touching and diagonally touching squares next to each numbered attractor. The particles travel only horizontally and vertically, and cannot pass through attractors. The beam cannot re-enter any square.

3				5			
							3
			7				4
	5						
				7			
3		7				8	
				5			

GALACTIC EMPIRE
VISUAL PROCESSING

Each of the planets (indicated by dots) in the grid below controls a region of space that has rotational symmetry around the planet. Draw along the dashed grid lines to show the territorial borders of all of the planets. Every square should be in the territory of exactly one planet. See page 35 for an example region.

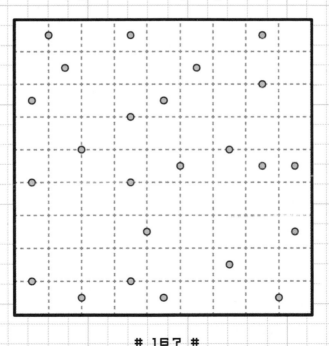

WATER WALKING

LATERAL HYPOTHESIS

Two scientists are discussing the possibility of miracles by the side of a lake.

One bets the other that she can walk across the surface of the lake using no special equipment.

Doubtful, the other takes her bet.

"Let's meet back here in four months' time," she says.

What is her plan?

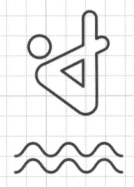

BINARY CODE
DEDUCTIVE LOGIC

Complete the binary matrix below by writing a "0" or a "1" into each empty square. Each row and column should contain four "0"s and four "1"s, and there should not be more than two "0"s or two "1"s in succession in any row or column.

					1	1	
0			0	1		1	1
		0			1	0	1
1				0			
			1				0
1	0	1			1		
0	1		0	1			1
	1	0					

169

SPACE RACE
DEDUCTIVE LOGIC

A star-class passenger ship is experiencing difficulties, and sends out a distress signal which is received by three galactic starships:

- The GSS Revelation
- The GSS Analysis
- The GSS Reconnaissance

These ships each travel at different speeds:

- One at ten light years per minute
- One at twelve light years per minute
- One at sixteen light years per minute

They are also different distances away:

- One is 120 light years away
- One is 140 light years away
- One is 160 light years away

Given that a) the Analysis is farther away than the ship that travels at twelve light years per minute, b) the ship that is 140 light years away is slower than the Revelation, and c) the name of the ship that travels at ten light years per minute begins with an "R", can you work out how soon each ship will arrive?

TWO BARS
NUMBER CRUNCHING

An iron bar and a steel bar together weigh 240 grams.

The iron bar weighs 120 grams less than the steel bar.

How much does the steel bar weigh?

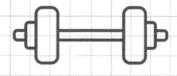

LOOP-THE-LAB
VISUAL PROCESSING

The laboratory below consists of a number of tiled floor areas, shown as white squares, and a number of permanent installations, shown as black squares. Can you find a route that visits every white square once and once only, then returns to the starting square? The route can only travel horizontally or vertically between squares.

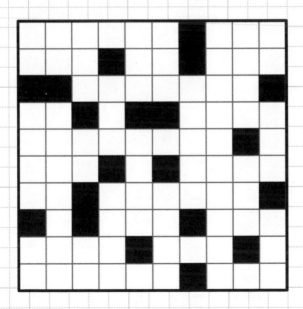

WRAPAROUND WIRING
VISUAL PROCESSING

The cables are missing between each of these pairs of sockets. Draw horizontal and vertical lines to indicate the route of each cable, so that each pair of numbers is linked. For electrical safety reasons, cables cannot cross either one another or a socket, and only one cable may enter any square. Cables may also plug into the edge of the board, in which case they can continue on the opposite end of the same row or column.

RING OF FIRE
NUMBER CRUNCHING

You have arranged a series of Bunsen burners in a perfect circle on the floor of the lab.

The 14th Bunsen burner is opposite the 42nd.

How many Bunsen burners are there in the circle?

CONNECTED CIRCUIT
DEDUCTIVE LOGIC

Connect all of the circled nodes with horizontal and vertical wires,
so that wires do not cross either each other or another node.
There may be zero, one, or two wires between each pair of nodes.
Each node should have the precise number of wires connected
to it as indicated by its number, and all of the nodes should be
connected so that current can flow from any node to any other
node simply by following one or more wires.

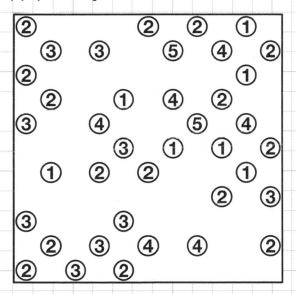

LAB LIGHTS
VISUAL PROCESSING

Can you work out the location of the lights on the lab plan below?
You know that every square of the lab must be illuminated by at
least one light, but also that no light illuminates any other light.
Due to the special lights used, they only light up squares in the
same row or column, and only as far as the first shaded square.
Some shaded squares contain numbers, revealing the number of
lights in the squares immediately to the left, top, right, and bottom.

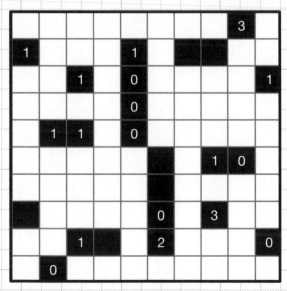

BIRTH OF EINSTEIN
NUMBER CRUNCHING

During a research project you learn that Albert Einstein was born in 1879.

You decide to see what numbers you can make using 1, 8, 7, and 9 in that order and any mathematical operations you want.

You come up with the following numbers:

- 25

- 71

- 135

- 504

- 505

- 513

- 567

- 68,024,448

How did you get them?

BLACK-OUT EXPERIMENT
DEDUCTIVE LOGIC

A particular experiment requires the careful configuration of six different variables into sets of five items. Add numbers to the diagram below so that each row, column and bold-lined 3×2 box contains five of the numbers in the range 1 to 6, with one per square. Shaded squares are "blacked out" and should not have a number written into them.

CHILL PILLS

DEDUCTIVE LOGIC

You have three types of pill to take each day:

- Red pills
- Blue pills
- Green pills

You are meant to take them at different times:

- One type before breakfast
- One type before lunch
- One type before dinner

You are also meant to take different amounts of each:

- 1 × 200mg of one
- 2 × 200mg of one
- 1 × 500mg of one

Given that a) you are meant to take the red type before the 2 × 200mg type, b) you are meant to take fewer mg of the dinner type than the green type, and c) you are only meant to take one blue pill per day, can you deduce how much you should take of which pill and when?

COMMON PROPERTY

LATERAL HYPOTHESIS

Over the course of several experiments, you notice that some of your results contain numbers with a particular property.

The numbers are as follows:

- 1,210

- 2,020

- 42,101,000

- 6,210,001,000

What is the common property these numbers share?

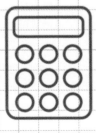

CELL REJECTION
DEDUCTIVE LOGIC

You need to set up an experiment whereby six different types of cell, A to F, are added to each row and column of a lab tray.

You must ensure that the cells do not interfere with one another. This means that two identical cells cannot be in grid squares that touch, including diagonally.

Can you place a cell into all the empty squares on the tray below?

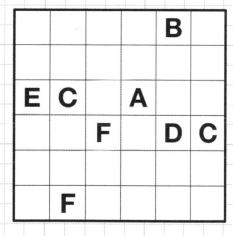

LAB MICE
VISUAL PROCESSING

You have built a maze to test the very smartest of your tame lab mice. Check that the maze is correctly constructed by finding a route from the entrance at the top to the exit at the bottom.

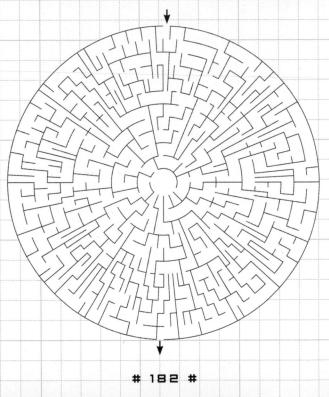

182

NO GREAT SHAKES
NUMBER CRUNCHING

You are attending a seminar and you notice that everyone shakes hands with everyone else.

You calculate that this means there will be 45 handshakes in total.

How many people are at the seminar?

BOTANIC CONFUSION
DEDUCTIVE LOGIC

A number of seeds are located beneath the soil of the plant bed shown below. Can you work out their exact locations? There is no more than one seed per square, and some squares are empty. No seed is in a numbered square. The numbers do, however, indicate the number of squares that contain seeds and which touch, including diagonally.

		0	0			3	1
	3						
2					3	5	
	3						2
	3					2	
2		5			2	2	
		3		2		2	
	2			1			

PERPLEXING PIPES
VISUAL PROCESSING

The piping system beneath your lab has been only partially constructed. Complete it by drawing in the missing pipes so that every square is connected into the pipe system, and it forms a single loop. Each square contains a corner segment, a straight segment, or a crossing segment. The pipes may only be placed horizontally and vertically, as shown.

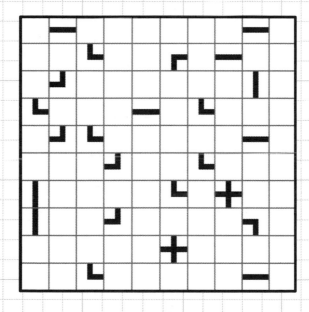

DEER IN HEADLIGHTS

REAL SCIENCE

You're driving fast down a country lane when you see a deer in the road up ahead.

You realize that it's not going to move before you reach it, so you will need to stop abruptly if you want to avoid hitting it.

Is your best bet to slam on the brakes or to brake gradually?

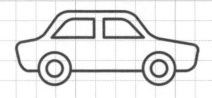

SOLUTIONS

SOLUTIONS

Page 8: Loop-the-Lab

Page 9: Engine Room

The one-engine plane. Having a second engine doubles the chance of engine failure.

Page 10: Phial Fitting

	3	5	1	2	2	
2	**2**	**1**	**5**	**4**	**3**	3
3	**3**	**2**	**4**	**1**	**5**	1
3	**1**	**3**	**2**	**5**	**4**	2
1	**5**	**4**	**3**	**2**	**1**	5
2	**4**	**5**	**1**	**3**	**2**	3
	2	1	4	2	3	

SOLUTIONS

Page 11: Component Connection

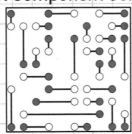

Page 12: Wheel Problem

Program the robot to remove one lug nut from each of the other three wheels and use them to reattach the fourth wheel to the rover. These should hold the wheels in place long enough for the robot to get back to the landing site.

SOLUTIONS

Page 13: Test Tube Test

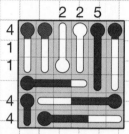

Page 14: Socket Pairs

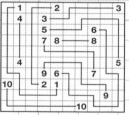

Page 15: Thin Ice

It would be easier to skate on ice that is -2°C because at this temperature your skates will temporarily melt the ice as you skate over it, creating a lubricating layer of water.

SOLUTIONS

Page 16: Fuel Pods

32 Cubes. Counting the top layer as level 1, this is made up of: Level 1 cubes = 2. Level 2 cubes = 5. Level 3 cubes = 8. Level 4 cubes = 17.

Page 17: Different Reactions

The clear solution is mildly acidic and turns cloudy when water is added to it. The blue solution is mildly alkaline and has no reaction when water is added to it. The orange solution is strongly acidic and violently reacts to water.

Page 18: Good Egg

To make the egg float, you can stir salt into the water. This increases the mass of the water without having much effect on its volume, until the water is denser than the egg. To suspend the egg halfway, start with the glass half full and stir salt into it. Then put in the egg, and pour more water on top.

SOLUTIONS

Page 19: Cell Rejection

B	F	E	D	A	C
C	A	B	F	E	D
D	E	C	A	B	F
F	B	D	E	C	A
A	C	F	B	D	E
E	D	A	C	F	B

Page 20: Lab Lights

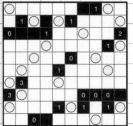

Page 21: Raise The Bar

The bigger bar is eight times heavier than the smaller bar.

SOLUTIONS

Page 22: Laboratory Logic

These are light bulbs, so they become hot when they are turned on. Go to the storage room, turn on two switches and wait a minute. Then turn off one switch and go into the lab. You will see one light is on, corresponding to the switch that you left on. You will see two lights that are off, one of which is hot and one of which is cold. By touching them, or moving your hand near them, you can work out which corresponds to the switch you turned on and then off, and which corresponds to the switch you did not turn on at all.

Page 23: Experimental Extension

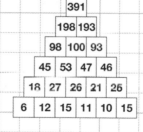

SOLUTIONS

Page 24: Sample Selection

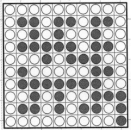

Page 25: A Striking Result

Eight seconds. The timing starts from the first strike, so there must be four seconds between strikes.

Page 26: Sails Pitch

No, the fan would propel the boat backward. This is because much of the wind created by the fan would not be caught by the sails, thus outweighing the forward propulsion of the wind hitting the sails.

SOLUTIONS

Page 27: Wiring Up

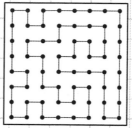

Page 28: Calculator Conundrum

Press: $-9 \div 9 + 9$

Page 29: Waste Disposal

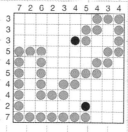

SOLUTIONS

Page 30: Mixture Mix-Up

The probability is zero. If you have put nine pieces of card in the right place, then the tenth must also be in the right place.

Page 31: Strange Attractors

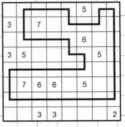

Page 32: Binary Code

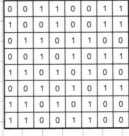

SOLUTIONS

Page 33: Experimental Extension

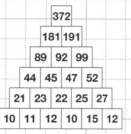

Page 34: Connected Circuit

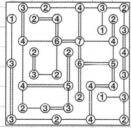

SOLUTIONS

Page 35: Galactic Empire

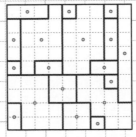

Page 36: Last Minute

Yes. Turn over both hourglasses. When (after five minutes) the five-minute hourglass runs out, turn it over again. When (after eight minutes) the eight-minute hourglass runs out, turn it over again. When (after ten minutes) the five-minute hourglass runs out again, the eight-minute hourglass has been running for two minutes. Turn it over again and when it runs out, twelve minutes will have passed.

SOLUTIONS

Page 37: Perplexing Pipes

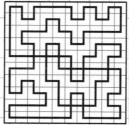

Page 38: Different Attractions

The bar magnet is the strongest and is made from alnico. The horseshoe magnet is the weakest and is made from ferrite. The ring magnet is of medium strength and is made from samarium cobalt.

Page 39: Power Trip

800 minutes. Each battery was used for four-fifths of the 1,000-minute total.

SOLUTIONS

Page 40: Phial Fitting

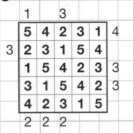

Page 41: Wraparound Wiring

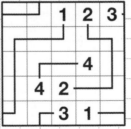

Page 42: Stop Cold

Input the figure as either Celsius or Fahrenheit. It doesn't matter which you put, as -40 degrees Celsius equals -40 degrees Fahrenheit.

SOLUTIONS

Page 43: Lab Mice

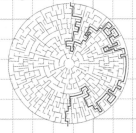

Page 44: Socket Pairs

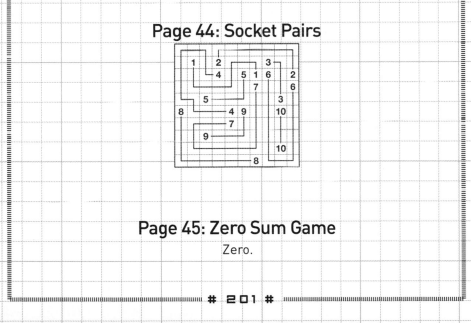

Page 45: Zero Sum Game

Zero.

SOLUTIONS

Page 46: Black-out Experiment

6	2		1	3	4
4	1	3		5	2
3		1	6	2	5
2	4	5	3	1	
1	5	4	2		6
	6	2	5	4	3

Page 47: Component Connection

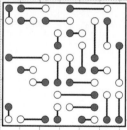

SOLUTIONS

Page 48: Up The Wrong Tree

Tie the rope around the tree on the shore of the lake. Then, holding one end of the rope, walk all the way around the lake, so that the rope is now around the tree on the island. Finally, tie the other end of the rope to the tree on the shore. The rope is now secure between the two trees, and can be used to get across to the island.

Page 49: Laser Mirrors

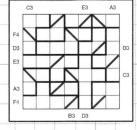

SOLUTIONS

Page 50: Botanic Confusion

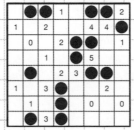

Page 51: Free Space

100 beakers. Call the number of beakers in the lab *a*. The original cupboard has room for (*a* - 20) beakers. When the capacity is multiplied by 1.5, it has room for (*a* + 20) beakers. Put mathematically, (*a* - 20) × 1.5 = (*a* + 20). Solving this by rearranging gives the answer: *a* = 100.

Page 52: Connected Values

5 ∘ 4	6 • 3 ∘ 2 • 1
6 1	4 • 2 5 3
4 ∘ 3 ∘ 2	5 1 6
3 ∘ 2 ∘ 1	6 4 ∘ 5
2 6 ∘ 5	1 3 • 4
1 5 3 ∘ 4	6 2

SOLUTIONS

Page 53: Wiring Up

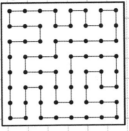

Page 54: Fuel Pods

43 cubes. Counting the top layer as level 1, this is made up of: Level 1 cubes = 4. Level 2 cubes = 7. Level 3 cubes = 13. Level 4 cubes = 19.

Page 55: Cell Rejection

A	E	C	D	F	B
F	B	A	E	C	D
C	D	F	B	A	E
B	A	E	C	D	F
E	C	D	F	B	A
D	F	B	A	E	C

Page 56: Loop-the-Lab

Page 57: Driven to Distraction

Your colleague drives twenty kilometers further than you do. To see this, choose any arbitrary length for the journey (of course, it must be over 30km) and calculate how far each of you would be driving.

SOLUTIONS

Page 58: Hidden Path

4 5 4 5 2 2

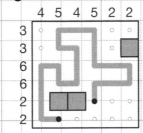

3
3
6
6
2
2

Page 59: The Beetles

The red beetle has seven spots and is 9mm long. The yellow beetle has eleven spots and is 6mm long. The brown beetle has twelve white spots and is 8mm long.

Page 60: Weight and See

A quarter of a pound. This becomes obvious if you imagine removing one bottle from each side, so you're left with two bottles weighing half a pound.

SOLUTIONS

Page 61: Diagonal Links

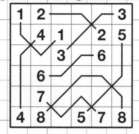

Page 62: Sample Selection

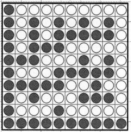

SOLUTIONS

Page 63: Experimental Extension

```
            253
         133 120
       75  58  62
     44  31  27  35
   25  19  12  15  20
 12  13   6   6   9  11
```

Page 64: Lab Lights

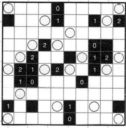

SOLUTIONS

Page 65: Waste Disposal

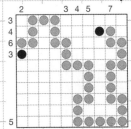

Page 66: Waxing and Waning

21. Burning the 64 would yield 16 more candles. Burning these sixteen would yield a further four, and burning these four would yield one more.

SOLUTIONS

Page 67: Binary Code

0	0	1	0	1	0	1	1
0	0	1	0	1	0	1	1
1	1	0	1	0	1	0	0
0	1	1	0	0	1	1	0
1	0	0	1	1	0	0	1
0	0	1	0	1	0	1	1
1	1	0	1	0	1	0	0
1	1	0	1	0	1	0	0

Page 68: Shaped Construction

G	E	D	F	B	C	A
A	G	E	B	C	F	D
F	D	A	E	G	B	C
B	A	C	G	D	E	F
C	F	G	A	E	D	B
D	B	F	C	A	G	E
E	C	B	D	F	A	G

SOLUTIONS

Page 69: On Another Planet

2ϖ meters, or approximately 6.28m. This is the difference between 2ϖr (the planet's circumference) and 2ϖ(r+1) (the journey of the hovercraft).

Page 70: Connected Circuit

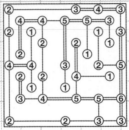

Page 71: Magnificent Measurement

60 degrees

SOLUTIONS

Page 72: Perplexing Pipes

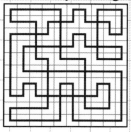

Page 73: Galactic Empire

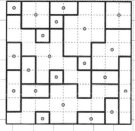

SOLUTIONS

Page 74: Mix and Match

No, the amount of saline solution in the beaker is the same as the amount of distilled water in the flask. This is because all the distilled water that is no longer in the beaker is now in the flask, and all the liquid that is not distilled water in the beaker is saline solution, and vice versa.

Page 75: Wraparound Wiring

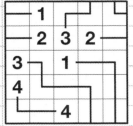

Page 76: Bird's-Eye View

Unlike humans, birds need gravity in order to swallow.

Page 77: Laser Mirrors

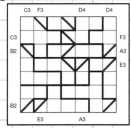

Page 78: Black-out Experiment

2	6	1	3		4
3		4	2	1	6
	5	2	1	4	3
4	1	3	6	5	
1	2		4	3	5
5	3	6		2	1

Page 79: An Alarming Problem

Approximately three hours. A wind-up alarm clock can only be set up to twelve hours in advance.

SOLUTIONS

Page 80: Strange Attractors

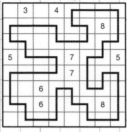

Page 81: Perfect Match

Bend the match to form an angle, and then the match's center of gravity will be in the bend and it will fall on its edge.

Page 82: Connected Values

$$
\begin{array}{cccccc}
5 \circ 6 \bullet 3 \circ 4 \bullet 2 \bullet 1 \\
4 \bullet 2 \bullet 1 \; 5 \circ 6 \bullet 3 \\
2 \; 5 \circ 6 \; 1 \; 3 \circ 4 \\
6 \; 1 \; 4 \circ 3 \; 5 \; 2 \\
3 \circ 4 \circ 5 \; 2 \bullet 1 \; 6 \\
1 \; 3 \circ 2 \; 6 \; 4 \circ 5
\end{array}
$$

SOLUTIONS

Page 83: Their Last Legs

Ten tripods and three clamp stands.

Page 84: Square Rooms

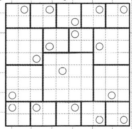

Page 85: Stone Cold

This apparent difference is explained by conduction. Carpet is a much worse conductor of heat than tiles, so when you step on the carpet it is slower to remove heat from your feet than tiles are, meaning it feels warmer.

SOLUTIONS

Page 86: Phial Fitting

	2				3	
	2	1	5	4	3	3
	5	3	4	1	2	
	4	2	3	5	1	2
	3	5	1	2	4	2
3	1	4	2	3	5	
	4		4			

Page 87: Dropping Off

Thirteen.

Page 88: Hidden Path

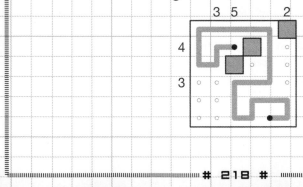

SOLUTIONS

Page 89: Plane Sailing

As is often the case, here the stalling is due to the plane flying too slowly, resulting in a lack of lift. The faster the plane dives, the more air flows over the wings, until eventually there is enough lift to enable the pilot to pull out of the dive.

Page 90: Shaped Construction

E	A	C	G	D	F	B
C	B	G	A	F	D	E
D	F	B	C	E	G	A
A	G	F	E	B	C	D
B	D	A	F	G	E	C
F	C	E	D	A	B	G
G	E	D	B	C	A	F

Page 91: Talking Sense

Two eyes allow for depth perception and let you estimate distances, while two ears help you determine from where a sound is coming. There is no such advantage from having two mouths.

SOLUTIONS

Page 92: Socket Pairs

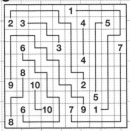

Page 93: Catch Your Breath

You should gradually let the air escape your mouth. This is because as you swim upward the pressure on your body decreases and the air in your lungs expands. To avoid rupturing your lungs, it is best to gradually release that air.

SOLUTIONS

Page 94: Lab Mice

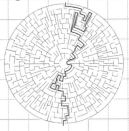

Page 95: Round Trip

The fly must be rotating twice as fast as the mirror.

Page 96: Fuel Pods

38 cubes. Counting the top layer as level 1, this is made up of: Level 1 cubes = 4. Level 2 cubes = 6. Level 3 cubes = 11. Level 4 cubes = 17.

Page 97: Just Graduated

Still the fifteen milliliter mark.

SOLUTIONS

Page 98: Loop-the-Lab

Page 99: Burst Your Bubbles

The high air pressure below ground kept the carbon dioxide in the cava in solution until you returned to the surface.

Page 100: Square Rooms

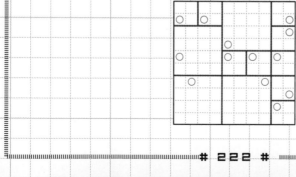

SOLUTIONS

Page 101: Diagonal Links

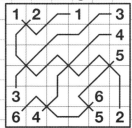

Page 102: Face The Music

Objects have a tendency to resonate at a particular frequency. Your finger causes the glass to vibrate until eventually the vibrations reach the natural frequency of the glass. This is when the glass sings. Your finger needs to be wet to reduce friction enough for it to reach to glass's frequency.

SOLUTIONS

Page 103: Waste Disposal

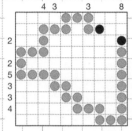

Page 104: Connected Circuit

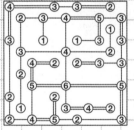

SOLUTIONS

Page 105: House-Warming Party

The percentage heat loss must always be 100%. Improving insulation will not reduce the percentage heat loss, as all heat will be lost eventually, but it can slow the rate of heat loss.

Page 106: Strange Attractors

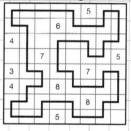

Page 107: Snow Business

Snow absorbs sound. Loosely packed snow in particular contains a lot of air gaps, making it more difficult for sound to bounce off the snow than off, say, water.

SOLUTIONS

Page 108: Shaped Construction

B	C	D	F	G	A	E
F	G	A	B	E	C	D
E	D	G	C	A	B	F
A	F	E	D	C	G	B
G	A	B	E	F	D	C
D	E	C	A	B	F	G
C	B	F	G	D	E	A

Page 109: Bunsen Squares

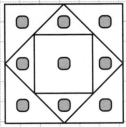

SOLUTIONS

Page 110: Lab Lights

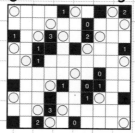

Page 111: In Hot Water

The noise is caused by bubbles that have been created by the heating element floating away into colder water and collapsing in on themselves. The noise stops when the kettle is about to boil because all the water is hot so the bubbles survive.

Page 112: Loop-the-Lab

Page 113: Find Your Voice

You're used to hearing your voice inside your head, via the vibrations of your skull. This gives it a lower sound than hearing it through your ears, which is how other people are used to hearing it.

SOLUTIONS

Page 114: Sample Selection

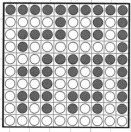

Page 115: Rock Fan

The igneous rock is the heaviest and you studied it on Wednesday. The metamorphic rock has the middle weight and you studied it on Monday. The sedimentary rock is the lightest and you studied it on Tuesday.

Page 116: On the Map

Yes. To see this, imagine taking your map to the region itself. Holding your smaller map while standing somewhere in the region, it is clearly certain that there is a point on the map you are holding which is the same as the point on which you are standing. The same principle holds for scales smaller than 1:1.

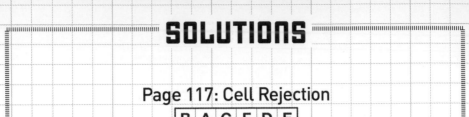

SOLUTIONS

Page 117: Cell Rejection

B	A	C	F	D	E
E	D	B	A	C	F
F	C	E	D	B	A
A	B	F	C	E	D
D	E	A	B	F	C
C	F	D	E	A	B

Page 118: Wiring Up

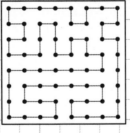

SOLUTIONS

Page 119: Break The Ice

The drinks are warmer than the ice. When you drop the ice cubes in, the outside of each cube warms up and expands, whereas the inside does not. This tension causes the crack.

Page 120: Binary Code

0	0	1	0	1	0	1	1
1	1	0	0	1	0	0	1
0	0	1	1	0	1	1	0
1	1	0	1	0	1	0	0
0	0	1	0	1	0	1	1
1	0	1	1	0	1	0	0
1	1	0	1	0	1	0	0
0	1	0	0	1	0	1	1

SOLUTIONS

Page 121: Component Connection

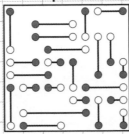

Page 122: Kidding Around

The probability that Alice's children are both boys is 1/3. The probability that Ben's children are both boys is 1/2.

Page 123: Experimental Extension

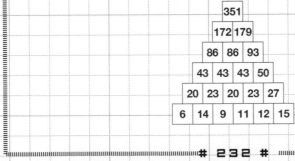

SOLUTIONS

Page 124: Diagonal Links

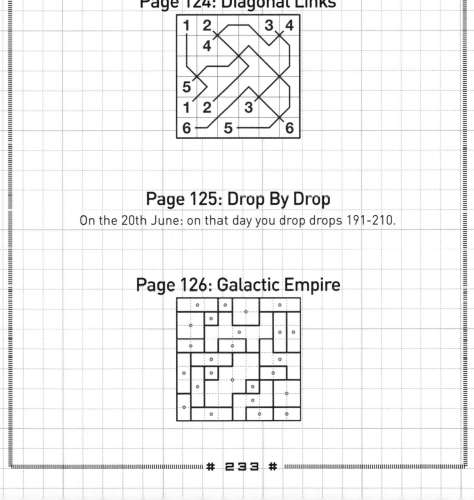

Page 125: Drop By Drop

On the 20th June: on that day you drop drops 191-210.

Page 126: Galactic Empire

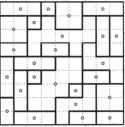

SOLUTIONS

Page 127: Earwigging

Pick out a small number of them, perhaps twenty. Then mark them with something like paint or correction fluid, and put them back in the crate. Once they've had a chance to reintegrate themselves, pick out another twenty. Let's say two of them are marked. Then you can infer that your original sample represented about 10% of the overall population. More repeats will make your estimate more reliable.

Page 128: Perplexing Pipes

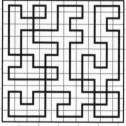

Page 129: The Late Report

No. If it has taken you twice as long as it should to write the first half of the report, then you're already out of time.

SOLUTIONS

Page 130: Wraparound Wiring

Page 131: The Breakdown

Thirty minutes. We know that decomposer A was able to break down 10/15 of the substance in ten minutes, meaning decomposer B must have broken down the other 5/15 in ten minutes. If 5/15 takes it ten minutes, then 15/15 would take it three times as long as that.

Page 132: Laser Mirrors

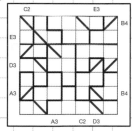

SOLUTIONS

Page 133: Time After Time

18 times faster. The tip of the hour hand moves $2 \times \pi \times 6$ centimeters every twelve hours, or π centimeters an hour. The tip of the minute hand moves $2 \times \pi \times 9$ centimeters every hour, or 18π centimeters an hour.

Page 134: Black-out Experiment

	2	3	1	5	6
1	6	5		3	4
6	3	1	5	4	
5	4		3	1	2
2	5	6	4		1
3		4	6	2	5

Page 135: Lab Mice

Page 136: Square Rooms

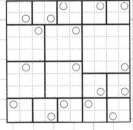

SOLUTIONS

Page 137: Hidden Path

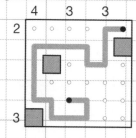

Page 138: Full Circle

Seven pieces. For example

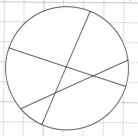

Page 139: Sponge Away

98%.

SOLUTIONS

Page 140: Double Time

On the first of August.

Page 141: Connected Values

5 ○ 4 • 2	6	1	3
2	5	1	3 • 6	4
3 ○ 2	5	1	4	6
4 ○ 3 • 6 ○ 5	2 ○ 1
1	6 • 3 ○ 4 ○ 5	2
6	1	4 • 2 ○ 3	5

Page 142: Shaped Construction

G	E	B	C	F	A	D
A	F	D	B	G	E	C
D	A	F	E	C	B	G
F	C	E	A	D	G	B
C	B	G	D	A	F	E
B	G	C	F	E	D	A
E	D	A	G	B	C	F

Page 143: Advanced Robotics

Cog is silver and needs two parts. Bolt is red and needs three parts.
Circuit is gold and needs four parts.

Page 144: The Weight Is Over

90 grams.

Page 145: Wiring Up

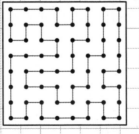

SOLUTIONS

Page 146: Phial Fitting

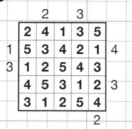

Page 147: Measure for Measure

Lie the bottle on its side. This makes it much easier to estimate halfway than if the bottle is standing up.

Page 148: Square Rooms

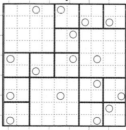

SOLUTIONS

Page 149: The Next Generation

None.

Page 150: Diagonal Links

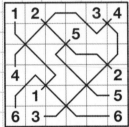

Page 151: Red Light

In a flash photograph the light flashes too fast for people's pupils to close, so a lot of bright light passes into the eye, reflects off the back of the eyeball and comes out again. The red is down to the choroid at the back of the eye, which contains a lot of blood. This can be avoided by pointing the flash away from the eyes, or preventing the picture's subjects from looking directly at the lens.

SOLUTIONS

Page 152: Sample Selection

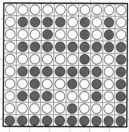

Page 153: Hidden Path

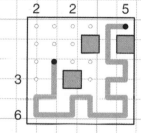

SOLUTIONS

Page 154: Chemical Separation

Pour the solution from the second test tube into the seventh test tube and then return it to its original position, then pour the solution from the fourth test tube into the ninth test tube and return it to its original position. The tubes will now alternate between full and empty.

Page 155: Connected Values

2 • 4 ○ 5	1	6 • 3
4 ○ 5	3 • 6	2 • 1
6	1 ○ 2	3 ○ 4 ○ 5
5 ○ 6	1	4 ○ 3 ○ 2
3 ○ 2	6 ○ 5	1	4
1	3 ○ 4 • 2	5 ○ 6

SOLUTIONS

Page 156: Socket Pairs

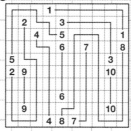

Page 157: Light Flask

Holes.

Page 158: Laser Mirrors

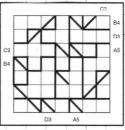

SOLUTIONS

Page 159: Alien Nations

The Sarpons have two eyes and one arm. The Melluans have no eyes and three arms. The Arrati have three eyes and two arms.

Page 160: Top Scientists

Yes, if the other 20% are all significantly below average. For example, let us say that 80% of scientists carried out twelve experiments this year, and the other 20% carried out two. In this case, the average is ten experiments, so 80% of scientists are above average.

Page 161: Component Connection

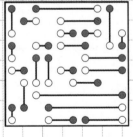

SOLUTIONS

Page 162: The Long Worm

Two tennis courts: after ten days, the worm is 5120 centimeters long, which is slightly more than the length of two tennis courts.

Page 163: Waste Disposal

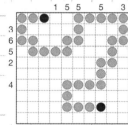

Page 164: Fuel Pods

36 cubes. Counting the top layer as level 1, this is made up of: Level 1 cubes = 3. Level 2 cubes = 5. Level 3 cubes = 12. Level 4 cubes = 16.

Page 165: The Strongest Acid

No, or else it would eat through the flask (and the floor, and so on).

SOLUTIONS

Page 166: Strange Attractors

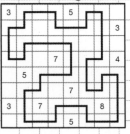

Page 167: Galactic Empire

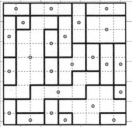

Page 168: Water Walking

She plans to wait until the lake has frozen over and then walk over it.

SOLUTIONS

Page 169: Binary Code

1	0	0	1	0	1	1	0
0	0	1	0	1	0	1	1
0	1	0	0	1	1	0	1
1	0	1	1	0	1	0	0
0	1	0	1	1	0	1	0
1	0	1	0	0	1	0	1
0	1	1	0	1	0	0	1
1	1	0	1	0	0	1	0

Page 170: Space Race

The GSS Revelation is 120 light years away and travels at twelve light years per minute, so will arrive in ten minutes. The GSS Analysis is 160 light years away and travels at sixteen light years per minute, so will arrive in ten minutes. The GSS Reconnaissance is 140 light years away and travels at ten light years per minute, so will arrive in fourteen minutes.

Page 171: Two Bars

180 grams.

Page 172: Loop-the-Lab

Page 173: Wraparound Wiring

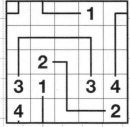

Page 174: Ring of Fire

56

SOLUTIONS

Page 175: Connected Circuit

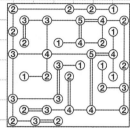

Page 176: Lab Lights

SOLUTIONS

Page 177: Birth of Einstein

$$25 = 1 + 8 + 7 + 9$$

$$71 = (1 \times 8) + (7 \times 9)$$

$$135 = 1 \times (8 + 7) \times 9$$

$$504 = 1 \times 8 \times 7 \times 9$$

$$505 = 1 + (8 \times 7 \times 9)$$

$$513 = (1 + (8 \times 7)) \times 9$$

$$567 = (1 + 8) \times 7 \times 9$$

$$68024448 = 18^7 / 9$$

Page 178: Black-out Experiment

6	2		1	5	4
4	5	1	6		3
5	1	3	4	2	
2		4	5	1	6
1	3	6		4	5
	4	5	2	3	1

SOLUTIONS

Page 179: Chill Pills

You are meant to take 1 × 500mg red pill before breakfast, 2 × 200mg green pills before lunch, and 1 × 200mg blue pill before dinner.

Page 180: Common Property

These numbers all describe themselves, in the sense that the first digit is how many zeros there are in the number, the second digit is how many ones there are, the third how many twos there are, and so on.

Page 181: Cell Rejection

C	D	E	F	B	A
F	A	B	C	E	D
E	C	D	A	F	B
A	B	F	E	D	C
D	E	C	B	A	F
B	F	A	D	C	E

SOLUTIONS

Page 182: Lab Mice

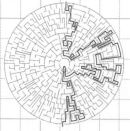

Page 183: No Great Shakes

Ten

Page 184: Botanic Confusion

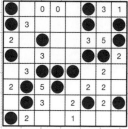

SOLUTIONS

Page 185: Perplexing Pipes

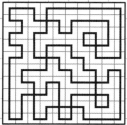

Page 186: Deer In Headlights

Your best bet is to brake very quickly but not instantly. If you brake instantly, your wheels may skid, which will impede your deceleration.